Praise for *Math Games for Geometry and Measurement* . . .

Students need math games that are challenging and engaging. However, finding quality learning stations that are mathematically rich and fun for students can be challenging. Jamee Petersen has made that easier for teachers by incorporating all of the characteristics of quality learning activities into this book. These games are the perfect match for anyone's math workshop and more.

— *Jennifer Lempp, educator and author of* Math Workshop: Five Steps to Implementing Guided Math, Learning Stations, Reflection, and More

As a classroom teacher, Jamee Petersen knows how important it is to provide hands-on, creative math experiences that enrich students' learning. Jamee's math games make the processes of acquiring geometry and measurement skills make sense. The organized layout of instructions, the simple materials needed, and the wealth of teaching tips make this a go-to resource for ensuring successful student learning.

— *Jill Borg, kindergarten teacher, Westonka Public Schools, Minnetrista, Minnesota*

What a fun and engaging way to positively impact student learning! The teacher-friendly format of this outstanding resource highlights the best of instructional practices, from learning targets and key questions to assessments. The games are highly engaging, connect to important math concepts, and promote deeper mathematical understanding.

— *Angee Luedtke, principal, Clinton Elementary, Lincoln, Nebraska*

Jamee has done it again! This thoughtful set of practical games is a brilliant way to help young students better understand the challenging concepts of geometry and measurement. Academic games are not only a well-researched strategy for engaging students but they also help solidify metacognitive skills like problem solving and critical thinking. Jamee's experiences as a classroom teacher and national mathematics trainer make her a reputable expert on this topic. Bravo, Jamee!

— *Tammy Heflebower, CEO of !nspire Consulting: Education and Business Solutions, Castle Rock, Colorado*

When teachers are pressed for time, having a resource like this is a life saver! Step-by-step directions, learning targets, and teaching tips help teachers bring these games to life in their classrooms. Jamee has done the hard work for teachers in identifying essential skills for geometry and measurement and creating engaging games to help develop those skills. This resource is a math teacher's best friend!

— *Kathleen Dial, principal, Imagine South Lake Charter School, Clermont, Florida*

MATH GAMES

for Geometry
and Measurement

Other Resources in This Series

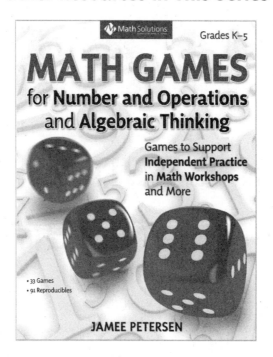

Math Games for Number and Operations and Algebraic Thinking, Grades K–5

Jamee Petersen

ISBN: 978-1-935099-43-7

MATH GAMES
for Geometry and Measurement

Games to Support
Independent Practice
in **Math Workshop**
and More

Math Solutions
Boston, Massachusetts, USA

JAMEE PETERSEN

Math Solutions
www.mathsolutions.com

Library of Congress Control Number: 2019943447

Math Solutions is a division of Houghton Mifflin Harcourt.

MATH SOLUTIONS® and associated logos are trademarks or registered trademarks of Houghton Mifflin Harcourt Publishing Company. Other company names, brand names, and product names are the property and/or trademarks of their respective owners.

Executive Editor: Jamie Ann Cross
Production Manager: Denise A. Botelho
Cover design: Vicki Tagliatela, DandiLion Design
Cover photo: (rolling red dice) ©MrJPEG/iStock/Getty Images / (silver numbers) ©skvoor/iStock/Getty Images
Author photo: Robert Photography
Interior design and composition: Susan Barclay, Barclay Design

Printed in the United States of America.

1 2 3 4 5 6 7 8 9 10   0304   27 26 25 24 23 22 21 20 19
4510006385   ABCDE

A Message from Math Solutions

We at Math Solutions believe that teaching math well calls for increasing our understanding of the math we teach, seeking deeper insights into how students learn mathematics, and refining our lessons to best promote students' learning.

Math Solutions shares classroom-tested lessons and teaching expertise from our faculty of professional learning consultants as well as from other respected math educators. Our publications are part of the nationwide effort we've made since 1984 that now includes:

- more than five hundred face-to-face professional learning programs each year for teachers and administrators in districts across the country;

- professional learning books that span all math topics taught in kindergarten through high school;

- videos for teachers and for parents that show math lessons taught in actual classrooms;

- on-site visits to schools to help refine teaching strategies and assess student learning; and

- free online support, including grade-level lessons, book reviews, inservice information, and district feedback, all in our Math Solutions Online Newsletter.

For information about all of the products and services we have available, please visit our website at *www.mathsolutions.com*. You can also contact us to discuss math professional learning needs by calling (877) 234-7323 or by sending an email to *info@mathsolutions.com*.

We're always eager for your feedback and interested in learning about your particular needs. We look forward to hearing from you.

Math Solutions.
FOUNDED BY MARILYN BURNS

From Houghton Mifflin Harcourt.

For MP and Blake

Contents

Two Ways to Find the Game You Want

Reproducibles and Other Downloadable Materials

Downloadable materials that accompany this resource can be accessed by registering your book at **www.mathsolutions.com/myonlineresources** using the key code MGGM. These materials include reproducibles, printable game directions, and connections to standards. To register your book, please follow these steps.

How to Access Online Materials

1. Go to **mathsolutions.com/myonlineresources** and log in if you already have an account. If you do not have an account, click or tap the Create New Account button at the bottom of the Log In form.

2. Create an account, even if you have created one with the Math Solutions bookstore. You will receive a confirmation email when your account has been created.

3. Once your account has been created, you will be taken to the Product Registration page. Click Register on the product you would like to access (in this case, *Math Games for Geometry and Measurement*).

4. Enter key code **MGGM** and click or tap the Submit Key Code button.

5. Click or tap the Complete Registration button.

6. To access the materials at any time, visit your account page.

KEY CODE: **MGGM**

Alphabetical List: Games Ordered Alphabetically by Title with Grade-Level Indication

Game	Recommended Grade Level						Page
	K	1	2	3	4	5	
1. Anything but Nothing! (Partitioning Shapes)			X	X			1
2. Area Stays the Same				X	X		8
3. Attributes Alike	X	X	X	X			12
4. Boxed In (A Game of Parallel and Perpendicular Moves)					X		18
5. Circle Up 360 (A Measurement Game Using Protractors)					X		24
6. Claim the Dots (Classifying Angles and Lines)					X		30
7. Compare (Geometry Version)	X	X					35
8. Compare (Measurement Version)	X	X	X				40
9. Connect Four (A Graphing Game)						X	46
10. Coordinates Secrecy (A Graphing Game)						X	51
11. Coordinate Tic-Tac-Toe				X	X	X	58
12. Desktop Shuffleboard (A Measurement Game)			X	X	X	X	64
13. Four Square (Plotting Points)						X	71
14. Geometry Go Fish			X	X			78
15. Go the Distance (Customary and Metric Versions)		X	X	X			82
16. Have to Halve (A Game of Partitioning)		X	X	X			88
17. Line Plot Tic-Tac-Toe			X				95
18. March to the Meter	X	X	X				101

Materials List: List of Games by Materials Used

Counters (chips, interlocking cubes, color tiles)

Game 2: Area Stays the Same

Game 6: Claim the Dots (Classifying Angles and Lines)

Game 8: Compare (Measurement Version)

Game 9: Connect Four (A Graphing Game)

Game 18: March to the Meter

Game 19: Mosaic (An Area Game)

Game 23: Volume 9

Dice

Game 1: Anything but Nothing! (Partitioning Shapes)

Game 5: Circle Up 360 (A Measurement Game Using Protractors)

Game 6: Claim the Dots (Classifying Angles and Lines)

Game 9: Connect Four (A Graphing Game)

Game 13: Four Square (Plotting Points)

Game 15: Go the Distance (Customary and Metric Versions)

Game 16: Have to Halve (A Game of Partitioning)

Game 17: Line Plot Tic-Tac-Toe

Game 18: March to the Meter

Game 19: Mosaic (An Area Game)

Game 21: Roll Fives to 60 (An Analog Clock Game)

Game 22: Sunshine (A Yahtzee-Like Game)

Game Boards

Game 4: Boxed In (A Game of Parallel and Perpendicular Moves)

Game 6: Claim the Dots (Classifying Angles and Lines)

Game 9: Connect Four (A Graphing Game)

Game 10: Coordinates Secrecy (A Graphing Game)

Game 11: Coordinate Tic-Tac-Toe

Game 13: Four Square (Plotting Points)

Game 17: Line Plot Tic-Tac-Toe

Game 19: Mosaic (An Area Game)

Game 21: Roll Fives to 60 (An Analog Clock Game)

Geoboards

Markers or Colored Pencils

Measurement Tools (ruler, protractor, meter stick)

Notecards

Paper Clips

Paper Plates or Cups

Pattern Blocks

continued

Materials List: List of Games by Materials Used, continued

Playing Cards or Customized Cards

Game 2: Area Stays the Same

Game 3: Attributes Alike

Game 7: Compare (Geometry Version)

Game 8: Compare (Measurement Version)

Game 12: Desktop Shuffleboard (A Measurement Game)

Game 14: Geometry Go Fish

Game 20: Positions (Identifying and Describing Shapes)

Rubber Bands

Game 16: Have to Halve (A Game of Partitioning)

Spinners (also Paper Clips)

Game 4: Boxed In (A Game of Parallel and Perpendicular Moves)

Game 20: Positions (Identifying and Describing Shapes)

Game 22: Sunshine (A Yahtzee-Like Game)

Paper and/or Pencil Only

Game 1: Anything but Nothing! (Partitioning Shapes)

Game 4: Boxed In (A Game of Parallel and Perpendicular Moves)

Game 9: Connect Four (A Graphing Game)

Game 10: Coordinates Secrecy (A Graphing Game)

Game 11: Coordinate Tic-Tac-Toe

Game 12: Desktop Shuffleboard (A Measurement Game)

Game 13: Four Square (Plotting Points)

Game 15: Go the Distance (Customary and Metric Versions)

Game 19: Mosaic (An Area Game)

Game 20: Positions (Identifying and Describing Shapes)

Game 22: Sunshine (A Yahtzee-Like Game)

Game 23: Volume 9

How to Use This Resource

What we want from children who play games is for them to construct insights into the games, create mathematical strategies for winning the games, explain those insights and strategies to others in their own words, have good reasons for believing in their insights and that their strategies work, and respond appropriately to challenges to the adequacy of those reasons and strategies. **These are important skills to acquire not only for mathematics but also in life in general.**

—Michael S. Schiro, Associate Professor,
Boston College and author of numerous games articles

Why These Games?
The Selection Process

The games in this resource have been selected carefully through a three-step process:

1. First, each game was chosen for its success, time and time again, in helping students develop skills in the mathematical areas of geometry and measurement (including data). In *Math Games for Geometry and Measurement* you will find all-time favorites such as *Connect Four* and *Compare*. You will also find games you've likely not encountered before, as well as twists on some of your personal favorites.

2. Second, the list of games was narrowed to those games that can be played successfully by learners on their own in learning stations as part of math workshop.

3. Third, every game was considered carefully within the context of mathematical standards, resulting in those that strongly support mathematical standards. For those who would like support with these connections, see page ix to download supporting materials.

My Story

When I first began teaching, I was constantly looking for resources to support my students' learning of mathematics. My search often led me to Math Solutions' publications. In later years, I became a consultant for Math Solutions. As I led professional learning courses across the nation, I found that much of my time was dedicated to developing capacity and depth in the areas of geometry, measurement, and data. Teachers near and far wanted ways to support their learning as well as their students' learning in these areas.

After facilitating professional learning for implementing math workshop, I developed and wrote *Math Games for Number and Operations and Algebraic Thinking*. This resource has helped teachers effectively introduce concepts while supporting individual learners and learning styles. There were two more strands of mathematics unaddressed in the first book, and so *Math Games for Geometry and Measurement* needed to be written. This book is a companion to the first. The more than twenty games in this book offer teachers an

> The more than twenty games in this book offer teachers an abundance of ideas for use in their learning stations during math workshop, while simultaneously providing meaningful practice and supporting individual students.

abundance of ideas for use in their learning stations during math workshop, while simultaneously providing meaningful practice and supporting individual students. *Math Games for Geometry and Measurement* supports teachers in differentiating any math curriculum by altering content, process, or product. Students are able to learn at their own level. Students are able to produce different products to demonstrate their understanding. Teachers are able to address the mathematical standards in geometry, measurement, and data. I collected and created these games, tested them with students, and *Math Games for Geometry and Measurement* includes them all.

Do I Have Time for These Games?

The instruction of each game takes approximately one math lesson or sixty minutes (some are slightly less than an hour and others are slightly more). The independent play of each game takes twenty to thirty minutes on average. It's important to note that every game is designed so students can ultimately play them independently, freeing you for time to do small-group instruction and more.

Do These Games Support My Curriculum?

The games offered within this resource support and sustain a math workshop model while complementing any math curriculum. The games support common mathematical standards as well (see page ix for directions on how to access and download these connections).

How Is This Resource Organized?

Step-by-Step Instructions

The format of this resource is intended to be friendly and accessible for you, the teaching professional. Each game features step-by-step instructions, organized in four steps:

Part I: The Connection: Relate the game to students' ongoing work.

Part II: The Teaching: Introduce and model the game to students.

Part III: Active Engagement: Engage students to ensure they understand how to play the game.

Part IV: The Link: Students play the game independently.

These steps are adapted from the Math Solutions resource *From Reading to Math: How Best Practices in Literacy Can Make You a Better Math Teacher* by Maggie Siena (2009).

Tips

Various tips are included in the margins of each game for quick reference; these tips are intended to facilitate the teaching of the game and give insights into managing game materials, how students might experience the game, how technology might assist when modeling the game, and more.

Key Questions

Every game includes key questions to ask students as you observe them playing. Asking these questions assists you in understanding how or whether students are developing strategies. By asking questions, students are given the opportunity to hear each other's thinking and to develop their own understanding of the content even further.

Learning Targets

Each game includes Learning Targets. The Learning Targets are guided by mathematical standards. They are written for the student in a way so that students have a clear understanding of the content knowledge required of them in the game. I recommend sharing Learning Targets and posting them where the class can easily see and refer to them as the game is played.

Differentiating Your Instruction and Assessments

Every game includes insights on how it can be modified according to the levels and needs of your students. Differentiation occurs when you alter content, process, or product. In some cases, assessments are also included.

Reproducibles

As often as possible, game materials—especially game boards and recording sheets—are provided in reproducible format at the end of this resource. As you might imagine, recording sheets encourage students to record their thinking; it is important for students to be able to articulate how they are thinking. It is equally valuable for other students to see how their partner is thinking about the content of geometry, measurement, and data. See page ix for directions on how to access and download the reproducibles.

Game Directions

At the end of the resource, you will find a condensed page of each game's directions written for students (these reproducibles are numbered starting with the letter G). These directions can be reproduced and handed out as needed to facilitate the game, especially during math workshop. The directions support students' success in playing each game and also make it easier for students to play the game at home. See page ix for directions on how to access and download printable versions of the game directions.

Get Started!

The games can be accessed in any order. To help you find the game you want as quickly as possible, two contents lists are provided:

This resource is written for professionals who wish to support students' understanding in learning about how mathematical concepts work. It's written to help students explore geometry, measurement, and data by using materials, engaging with peers, and discussing and deepening their understanding. This resource is written for us—the teachers and teaching professionals who want our students to succeed in mathematics. It is written with a love for learning, compassion for colleagues, and dedication to students past, present, and future. My hope is that *Math Games for Geometry and Measurement* enriches the understanding of your students while minimizing your planning and preparation time. It's all here. Use it. Enjoy it. Share it.

Anything but Nothing!
(Partitioning Shapes)

Overview

This game gets students actively engaged in partitioning shapes, a critical part of geometry standards in grades 2 and 3. The game is played with pattern blocks. Each player begins by placing three yellow hexagons in front of them. The goal of the game is for students to partition each of the three hexagons—one into halves, another into thirds, and the last into sixths—using the trapezoid, rhombus, and triangle pattern blocks. Each player, when it's their turn, rolls a fraction die to determine what pattern block to use to cover a hexagon. A hexagon can only be covered by the same size and shape pattern blocks. The first player to fully partition (cover) all three hexagons is the winner.

Materials

- pattern blocks, 1 set per student: 3 yellow hexagons, 2 red trapezoids, 3 blue rhombuses, 6 green triangles

- *Anything but Nothing!* fraction die (a die with six faces labeled: $\frac{1}{2}, \frac{1}{3}, \frac{1}{3}, \frac{1}{6}, \frac{1}{6}$ and the last face is blank), 1 per group of students

- *Anything but Nothing!* Game Directions (REPRODUCIBLE G-1), 1 per group of 2–4 students

Related Game

Game 3: Attributes Alike

Recommended Grades 2–3

Time   Instruction: 45–60 minutes
Independent Play: 20–30 minutes

 TIME SAVERS
Creating Pattern Block Sets

For this game students will only be utilizing four of the six pattern blocks that come in a standard pattern block kit. Sort out the tan rhombus and the orange square from the kits prior to the lesson, or you might use the exploration time described in Step 1 of the lesson for students to separate the pattern blocks so that students have just the yellow hexagons, red trapezoids, blue rhombuses, and green triangles available to them (see Figure 1.1).

Figure 1.1. The pattern block shapes for use in this game.

Managing Materials

For ease in managing the distribution of materials, keep the pattern block sets in quart-size sandwich bags and the game directions in student binders or folders. Everything can then be stored in students' desks or cubbies for easy retrieval, especially for independent practice.

Don't Have Dice?

If you do not have the dice required for this game, use cards marked with the necessary fractions. Instead of rolling dice, players draw a card when it is their turn.

LEARNING TARGETS

Post the game's Learning Targets for students to see. This helps reinforce what students are responsible for learning as they play the game.

Grade 2:

- I can partition shapes into two and four equal shares.

- I can describe the shares using the words *halves, fourths,* and *quarters.*

- I can use the phrases *half of, fourth of,* and *quarter of.*

Grade 3:

- I can partition shapes into parts with equal area.

- I can express the area of each part as a fraction of the whole.

TEACHING TIP
Think-Pair-Share

Consider using a think-pair-share during *The Connection* piece of the lesson. This strategy is brain compatible, engaging, and found in *Thinking Strategies for Student Achievement,* a recommended book of the National Urban Alliance by Denise Nessel and Joyce Graham (2006). Think, pair, share is a strategy designed for getting students actively involved in the lesson through interaction. After posing the prompt *"Think* about other food that is partitioned," students think quietly to themselves about their ideas. After a bit of wait time, students *pair* with another classmate to discuss their ideas. Lastly students *share* their thinking with the rest of the class. This final step is typically teacher-facilitated for efficiency.

Key Questions

- How many halves make a whole?

- How many fourths make a whole?

- What portion of the trapezoid does this piece represent? (Ask this while holding a trapezoid or rhombus pattern block in hand.)

Teaching Directions
Part I: The Connection
Relate the game to students' ongoing work.

Before starting this game, encourage students to connect math to their life. Bring in a food item such as a graham cracker or club cracker. Discuss how the manufacturer scored the cracker into fourths. Use language like, "the whole cracker is partitioned or divided into fourths." Have students lead a similar discussion for a few other foods that are partitioned.

Part II: The Teaching
Introduce and model the game to students.

1. Have students used pattern blocks before? If students have not yet used pattern blocks or if it has been some time in using them, start with a brief pattern block exploration (for an idea of what this exploration might be, see the Creating Pattern Block Sets tip next to the list of materials).

2. Explain to students that they will be playing the game *Anything but Nothing!* in groups of two to four. Ask students to first gather around a demonstration area such that each student has table space to work.

3. Distribute the sets of pattern blocks, customized per the "Materials" list, one set per student. Ask students to find one hexagon in their set and place it in front of them.

4. Next ask students to select two trapezoids from their pattern block sets.

5. Show how two trapezoids, when placed precisely, cover up the entire hexagon. Explain, "We call this partitioning. The hexagon has been portioned into two parts. The two trapezoid pieces each represent a half of the hexagon."

6. Now have students move the hexagon covered in trapezoids to the side of their working space.

7. Instruct students to place two more hexagons in front of them. Ask, "Find other pattern blocks in your set that can be used to partition each hexagon. You must use pattern blocks of the same size and shape for the entirety of each hexagon."

8. As students begin to explore which pieces will cover an entire hexagon, circulate, ensuring that students are using pattern blocks of the same size and shape to partition each hexagon.

9. After a minute or so, most students will have determined that three blue rhombuses can be placed to partition one hexagon into thirds and six green triangles can be used to divide the other hexagon into sixths:

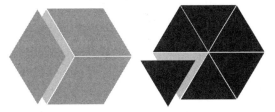

Figure 1.2. How students might partition their hexagon.

10. Again, have students move these covered hexagons to the side.

11. Have students ideally form groups of three. The game may be played in groups of two to four but three works well for the demonstration portion of the lesson, as students can help coach each other while still remaining actively engaged.

TEACHING TIP
Addressing Multiple Learning Styles
Students learn best in a variety of ways. Incorporating multiple styles of learning into any lesson increases student attentiveness and understanding. In Steps 11–16 of this lesson, students use several senses— seeing, hearing, and touching—to learn.

12. Next, introduce students to the fraction die (see "Materials" list); give a die to each group. Ask students to become familiar with the faces on their die.

13. Review the faces of the die. Have students find the face marked $\frac{1}{2}$. Ask, "Which pattern block represents one-half of a hexagon?"

14. Repeat Step 13 for the die faces $\frac{1}{3}$ and $\frac{1}{6}$.

15. Next explain what the die side with nothing (the blank side) means for this game. Say, "The name of the game is called *Anything but Nothing!* for a very good reason. When it is your turn and you roll the die, if nothing comes up on the first roll, you do just that—nothing! The turn goes to the next player. If you roll the die on a consecutive turn and nothing comes up, you have to remove all the pattern block pieces you have collected up to this point, so you are left with three hexagons with nothing on them."

16. Next, distribute the *Anything but Nothing!* game directions (REPRODUCIBLE G-1) to each student. Have students read the directions to themselves and then ask for a few volunteers to read the directions aloud as a class.

17. Proceed to modeling the game. To do this, gather students around a large table or floor space. Make sure all students can see the demonstration.

18. Make sure you have a set of pattern blocks in your demonstration space. Place the three hexagons in front of you and move the remaining pattern blocks (trapezoids, rhombuses, and triangles) to a nearby pile.

19. Ask for a student volunteer, Player 2, to demonstrate the game with you. Give him a set of pattern blocks and have him arrange the blocks as you did with your set in Step 18.

20. Roll the fraction die. If nothing comes up, do nothing. If $\frac{1}{2}$ comes up, select a trapezoid from

TEACHING TIP
Arranging Students
For the modeling part of this game, have students make two concentric circles. In the first circle, students kneel or sit; in the second, students stand. This ensures that everyone can view the demonstration area.

TECHNOLOGY TIP
Using an Interactive Whiteboard
If whiteboard technology is available, create a page with three hexagons near the top and a trapezoid, rhombus, and triangle near the bottom. These shapes can all be found in the mathematics tool kit. Infinitely clone the trapezoid, rhombus, and triangle to allow for multiple pattern block pieces to be pulled up and over the hexagons as you demonstrate partitioning.

your set and place it on top of the hexagon. Point out how this partitions the hexagon into halves. Should $\frac{1}{3}$ be rolled, take a rhombus and place it on the second hexagon. Show how this partitions the hexagon into thirds. If $\frac{1}{6}$ is rolled, select the triangle pattern block and place it on top of the third hexagon to illustrate that hexagon divided into sixths.

21. Initiate a conversation with students: "What should my next move be?" Explain that as Player 1 you have two choices: "I can stop and be finished with my round or I can roll again. I am taking a risk if I roll again. If I roll the side with nothing (the blank side), I have to remove all pattern block pieces that are covering up the hexagons and start over with nothing."

22. Rolling again is great for demonstration and will result in one of two scenarios: (1) you roll a fraction that can be used to partition the same or another hexagon depending on the number previously rolled, or (2) you will roll nothing and have to clear all your hexagons.

23. Figure 1.3 shows an example of a game where Player 1 (the teacher) rolled three times before deciding to end her turn and pass the die to Player 2. The three rolls were: $\frac{1}{6}$, $\frac{1}{2}$, and $\frac{1}{6}$. Hence the player placed pattern blocks over his three hexagons accordingly: the triangle pattern block ($\frac{1}{6}$) over the third hexagon, the trapezoid pattern block ($\frac{1}{2}$) over the first hexagon, and another triangle pattern block ($\frac{1}{6}$) over the third hexagon. This leaves the second hexagon empty; it will ultimately have three rhombuses in it to partition it into thirds.

Figure 1.3 Player 1's three moves after rolling $\frac{1}{6}$, $\frac{1}{2}$, and $\frac{1}{6}$.

 TEACHING TIP
Think Out Loud
As a volunteer student and you demonstrate the game, make sure you are both thinking out loud. This will help students see your thinking, learn the game, and understand the decisions being made.

TEACHING TIP
Formative Assessment
Formative assessments are necessary to gauge student understanding. They may be used before, during, or after a lesson. In the case of demonstrating this game, a formative assessment is recommended to determine if students are ready to play independently. Consider the assessment thumbs-up. Ask students, "Do you feel you understand the game enough to play on your own?" Have students put their thumbs up to indicate, "Yes, I completely understand. I know this," and thumbs down if "No, I need more time. I don't understand all the steps yet." Students may also show a thumbs-out to indicate uncertainty, "I mostly understand, however I need to see a bit more demonstration."

TEACHING TIP
Managing Classroom Noise
To diminish the noise of die being rolled and pattern blocks being moved throughout the game, use padded work spaces. A carpet square on the floor or a foam/fabric placemat on a desk or table alleviates some of the noise as well as provides a definitive work area.

24. When it is Player 2's turn, have him roll the die, select the pattern block that represents the fraction rolled, and place it on one of his hexagons.

25. Determine if students have grasped the game by using a formative assessment technique (see Teaching Tip). The first player to fully partition all three hexagons is the winner. You may not need to complete an entire game of *Anything but Nothing!* for students to grasp the procedure.

Part III: Active Engagement
Engage students to ensure they understand how to play the game.

26. Have students work in the same groups of three that they were in for Step 11. Each group should have a fraction die. Each student should have a set of pattern blocks, with the three hexagons placed in front of them and the remaining pattern blocks in a pile near them.

27. As students are playing, circulate, making sure to observe each group and ask questions. Questions fall into two categories: procedural and conceptual. Procedural questions are those that determine the student's understanding of how the game is played. Conceptual questions are those that address the geometry standards being practiced. For the latter, you might ask, "How are you partitioning this hexagon?" Or, "If the hexagon is the whole in this game, what fractional part of the hexagon does a trapezoid represent?"

28. It is important for students to have enough time to experience all of the scenarios of the game. Because the game incorporates both skill and luck, students will finish a game at varying times. Providing around 15 minutes for this portion of the lesson should be sufficient.

Part IV: The Link
Students play the game independently.

29. Set students up for independent practice with the game. Each group of students should have pattern block sets (one per student) and a copy of the *Anything but Nothing!* Game Directions as needed (REPRODUCIBLE G-1). Circulate while students are engaged with the game to ensure students are both on task and learning the skill being practiced.

TEACHING TIP
Displaying Game Directions
Consider making additional copies of the directions and post them throughout the classroom for students to refer to during independent play.

MATH WORKSHOP AND SUMMARIZING THE EXPERIENCE
Teach this game at the beginning of the week to the whole class, then make it an integral part of your math workshop (for more on math workshop, see *Math Workshop* by Jennifer Lempp). Build in time to observe students playing the game. Note their individual skill level and the strategies being utilized; come together later in the week and demonstrate their learning with the pattern blocks. Then apply the concept of $\frac{1}{2}$, $\frac{1}{3}$ and $\frac{1}{6}$ to other items in the classroom or around the school building.

ASSESSMENT
Partitioning
After students have had many experiences playing the game over a period of a week or the time allotted for addressing the geometry standard, consider using the *Anything but Nothing!* Assessment (REPRODUCIBLE 1) to measure acquisition and depth of knowledge.

Area Stays the Same

Recommended Grades 3–4
Time Instruction: 30–45 minutes
Independent Play: 15–20 minutes

LEARNING TARGETS

Post the game's Learning Targets for students to see. This helps reinforce what students are responsible for learning as they play the game.

Grade 3:
- I can reason with shapes and their attributes.
- I understand concepts of area and relate area to multiplication and addition.

Grade 4:
- I can solve problems involving measurement and conversion of measurements.

TIME SAVERS

A Deck of Cards
For the purpose of this game, a deck is 30 cards (1 copy of Reproducible 2, front and back).

Reusable Cards
To ensure the longevity of cards, use thick paper stock and/or laminate them. Store each deck in a sandwich bag.

Color-Coding Decks
To keep decks of cards from getting mixed up with other sets, use a different color of paper for each deck.

Overview
This game actively engages students in identifying arrays of the same area. *Area Stays the Same* cards (REPRODUCIBLE 2) are scattered about the playing space much like you would see them in a game of *Go Fish*. Players take turns selecting two cards they believe show arrays with the same area. If correct, the player keeps the cards. If incorrect, the player returns the cards to the playing space. Once all the cards have been matched, the player with the most cards wins.

Materials
- color tiles, approximately 10 per student
- *Area Stays the Same* Cards (REPRODUCIBLE 2, front and back), 1 deck per pair of students
- *Area Stays the Same* Game Directions (REPRODUCIBLE G-2), 1 per pair of students

Related Game
Game 19: Mosaic (An Area Game)

Key Questions
- How are you determining the area of the arrays?
- Apply the formula for area to this rectangle. Explain your thinking as you do this.
- What is the multiplication equation that describes the area of this rectangle? Explain your thinking.
- If we placed these two rectangles side by side, what would the area of the new shape be? Why?

Teaching Directions

Part I: The Connection

Relate the game to students' ongoing work.

Ask each student to grab a handful of color tiles (or distribute approximately 10 tiles to each student). Task each student with making an array using just four tiles. Discuss the two different orientations and configurations: 1 by 4 and 2 by 2. Show students the two cards that have matching arrays. Repeat with a different number of tiles like six or nine and show the two cards with matching arrays.

Part II: The Teaching

Introduce and model the game to students.

1. Explain to students that they will be playing the game *Area Stays the Same* in pairs. Ask students to first gather around a demonstration area.

2. Place the cards, array side up, in the middle of the demonstration area. Spread them out so that all the cards can be seen.

3. Tell students they are looking for two cards showing arrays with the same area. Remind them of how they created arrays with the same area using tiles.

4. Suggest looking for the two cards showing arrays with the area of four (1 by 4 and 2 by 2), the first array they tiled.

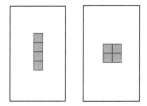

5. Once students select the two cards, flip the cards over to confirm that the areas match, and if so, then place the pair of cards aside.

6. Ask students to look for other pairs that they think have the same area.

TEACHING TIPS

Reviewing Mathematical Vocabulary

Some students may need a review of the term *array*. An array is items arranged in rows and columns. Demonstrate this with items in the classroom like student desks, index cards or green square pattern blocks. If graph paper is available, have the students cut out two arrays that have the same area.

The Importance of Asking Questions

Asking students how they are determining the area of the arrays provides insight as to where students are on the continuum for linking addition and multiplication concepts. Some students may count each individual square, while others might count a row and then count by that number for the number of columns; still others may count one row and one column and then multiply the two numbers. Learning this is useful when grouping students for playing the game as well as determining small groups for guided instruction.

TEACHING TIP

Arranging Students

For the modeling part of this game, have students make two concentric circles. In the first circle, students kneel or sit; in the second, students stand. This ensures that everyone can view the demonstration area.

TEACHING TIPS
Mixing Up the Cards
If students have previously played the game of *Tens Go Fish* featured in *Math Games for Number Operations and Algebraic Thinking*, or the traditional game of *Go Fish*, they may have varying ideas about when to mix up the cards. Some will want to mix the cards up after each round, others may want to mix the cards up each time a player is incorrect and returns cards, and yet others may want to only mix the cards at the beginning of the game. There is no right way; however, have pairs of students determine their way at the beginning of the game.

Formative Assessment
Formative assessments are necessary to gauge student understanding. They may be used before, during, or after a lesson. In the case of demonstrating this game, a formative assessment is recommended to determine if students are ready to play independently. Consider the assessment thumbs-up. Ask students, "Do you feel you understand the game enough to play on your own?" Have students put their thumbs up to indicate, "Yes, I completely understand. I know this," and thumbs down if "No, I need more time. I don't understand all the steps yet." Students may also show a thumbs-out to indicate uncertainty, "I mostly understand, however I need to see a bit more demonstration."

7. Collect two more cards that students have helped select as having arrays with the same area. Flip them over to confirm the areas match, and if so, place the pair of cards to the side.

8. Explain that in this game, each player gets a turn to select two cards they believe show arrays with the same area. If correct, students keep the cards. If incorrect, students return both cards to the playing area.

9. Determine if students have grasped the game by using a formative assessment technique (see Teaching Tip). Explain that when all the cards have been matched up, players count their pairs of cards. The player with the most pairs wins that round.

Part III: Active Engagement
Engage students to ensure they understand how to play the game.

10. Now give students the opportunity to explore the game in pairs. Each pair should have a set of cards.

11. As students are playing, circulate, noting how they are determining if the arrays do indeed have the same area. Keep in mind that students will have a wide variety of ways of determining the area.

12. For the *Active Engagement* part of the lesson, place a time limit on the game. When the timer goes off and once both players have had an equal number of turns, have students end the play at that point and count their cards to determine who had more matches.

Part IV: The Link
Students play the game independently.

13. Set students up for independent practice with the game. Each pair of students should have a set of cards and a copy of the *Area Stays the Same* Game Directions as needed (REPRODUCIBLE G-2).

14. Think about how students will be held accountable for practicing this game. This might be a class log sheet posted next to the materials bin. This is an example from one classroom:

Array	Array	Area Stays the Same
		$1 \times 4 = 4$ $2 \times 2 = 4$
		$1 \times 6 = 6$ $2 \times 3 = 6$

MATH WORKSHOP AND SUMMARIZING THE EXPERIENCE

Teach this game at the beginning of the week to the whole class, then make it an integral part of your math workshop (for more on math workshop, see *Math Workshop* by Jennifer Lempp). Have students partner up. Give each student ten color tiles as you did in the introduction of the game. This time, instruct each pair of students to create two different polygons that have the same area (area of 10). Let students know that they are not limited to regular polygons. Remind them the color tiles need to share a side. Note: If more color tiles are available in the classroom, pairs of students could choose a number greater than ten and demonstrate the concept of area stays the same. When doing this, place a limitation on how large the number can be. Use a range (e.g., ten to twenty color tiles per student). Hold a class discussion, prompting students to compare their polygons and further discuss how they know the areas are the same or different.

TEACHING TIPS
Pairing Students
See Teaching Tip "The Importance of Asking Questions" on page 9. Also consider students' learning styles when creating pairs for this game. Homogeneous grouping (grouping students with similar abilities) works well too. Some rounds of play may go more quickly for pairs who have a stronger skill set in computation and/or a preferred visual-spatial learning style. The speed of the game is only important in that students are working at a rate that suits their cognition. If this is students' first exposure to arrays and they are just embarking on the concepts of multiplication, consider first having them work in groups of four (two teams of two).

Emphasize Collaboration
For Part III, "Active Engagement," students should test the game out *with* their partner, not playing against him or her. The goal is for students to work together in understanding *how* to play the game and the math that is involved. When students have the opportunity to play the game independently (Part IV), they can play each other.

DIFFERENTIATING YOUR INSTRUCTION
Perimeter Stays the Same
One way to modify or extend the game according to the levels and needs of your students is to play the game using perimeter as the measurement that remains the same. For this version, do not print the cards back to back. Students scatter the cards number and array sides up and match the number with the array for a pair.

Attributes Alike

Recommended Grades K–3
Time Instruction: 45–60 minutes
Independent Play: 20–30 minutes

TIME SAVERS
A Deck of Cards
For the purpose of this game, a deck of cards is four copies of the three-page reproducible, each copy in a different color (i.e., blue, green, red, yellow). This means a deck will have 18 cards of each of the four colors, or 72 cards total.

Reusable Cards
To ensure the longevity of cards, use thick paper stock and/or laminate them. Store each deck in a sandwich bag.

Overview
This game is similar to the game of *Uno* in that students play cards that have attributes in common. Players take turns playing a card that has two attributes alike and one differing from the faceup card (attributes are color, shape, and size). If a player cannot play a card, she or he must draw one more card. Play continues until one player has played all their cards. This game addresses standards across several grade levels; kindergartners analyze and compare shapes (they may be ready for this game toward the end of the school year) whereas first, second, and third graders work toward reasoning with the attributes of shapes (rectangles, squares, trapezoids, and rhombuses).

Materials
- *Attributes Alike* Cards (REPRODUCIBLE 3), 1 deck per group of 2–4 students
- *Attributes Alike* Game Directions (REPRODUCIBLE G-3), 1 per group of 2–4 students

Related Games
Game 7: Compare (Geometry Version)

Game 14: Geometry Go Fish

Key Questions
- Point to the card you are considering playing next. Why is that a "good" card to play?
- How are you organizing the cards in your hand—by color, shape, or size of shape? If you are not organizing your cards, why not?

Teaching Directions
Part I: The Connection
Relate the game to students' ongoing work.

Bring in a deck of *Uno* cards and ask how many students have seen the game before. How many students have played it? Tell students that the game being introduced today is played similarly to *Uno*.

Part II: The Teaching
Introduce and model the game to students.

1. Prepare a deck of *Attributes Alike* Cards (REPRODUCIBLE 3) with the "wild cards" removed and set aside but available for later (Step 18).

2. Explain to students that they will be playing the game *Attributes Alike* in small groups. First, ask students to sit in a large circle on the rug. Once students are seated, hand each student a card from your prepared deck. Encourage students to keep their card in nice condition (they should refrain from bending or folding their card).

3. As you are distributing the cards, ask students to "Look at your card and be ready to describe it to others seated in the circle."

4. Ask students to describe their card out loud. Students will hopefully identify both the card's color and the shape featured on it (at this point they will not notice the size of the shape since they are only looking at one card and have not yet made any comparisons).

5. After a few students have shared, talk about the word *attribute*. Explain, "What you are sharing is called an *attribute*. Attributes are characteristics, traits, or properties. The attributes you are sharing fall into two different categories—color and shape."

6. Write the words *color* and *shape* where everyone can see them. Resume the sharing; as students describe their card, list the words

TEACHING TIP
Vocabulary
Many standards read that first graders should be able to reason with shapes and their attributes; standards also list rectangles, squares, and trapezoids as some of the quadrilateral shapes students should be able to distinguish between. In this game, a rhombus is also used. Introduce the word *rhombus* to students who might be searching for the correct term while describing their card.

TEACHING TIP
Comparing Sizes
Having students place their cards in order from largest shape to smallest shape will help promote discussion around similarities and differences in the attribute of size of the same shape.

they say under the appropriate heading. Your list will look something like this:

color	shape
blue	rectangle
green	rhombus
red	square
yellow	trapezoid

7. Next, divide students into four small groups. The shape that appears on their card determines which group they join: rectangles, squares, trapezoids, or rhombuses. Before students move into their groups, give them their task: "When you get into your alike-shape groups, compare your cards. What do you notice about them?"

8. Students move, confer, and discover that the shapes on the cards are of differing sizes.

9. Add the last heading, *size*, to your list.

10. Now explain that students are going to leave their groups in search of those who have the same-color card as them. They should then return to the whole-group circle, only this time sit so students with the same-color cards are next to them.

11. Once students have reassembled, take the remaining cards in your deck and stack them facedown in the center of the circle. Indicate that this is the "draw" pile. Draw the top card from the stack, flip it over, and place it faceup next to the stack—call this the start of the "discard" pile.

12. Ask, "Is anyone holding a card that has two of the same attributes as this card and one differing from this card (point to the card facing up)?"

13. Discuss which cards work and why. Select a student to "play" their card by placing it on top of the card facing up.

14. Now, using the new card facing up, ask students again, "Is anyone holding a card that has two of the same attributes as this card and one differing from this card (point to the card facing up)?"

15. Continue, repeating Steps 11–13, until students have a sense for how the game is played.

16. Now explain that in this game each player will begin with seven cards. Point out that "Sometimes you will not have a card that works. When that happens, you must draw the top card from the draw pile—the pile facing down."

17. Continue, "Should you draw a card that may be played, you may play it, otherwise it becomes part of your hand and play goes on to the next player."

18. Introduce the *wild card* (the cards you had originally set aside from your deck). Show students there are eight wild cards in each deck, two of each color. These may be used when the cards you are holding don't allow you to play; a wild card can be played anytime as long as you assign attributes (two of the same and one differing) to it.

19. Finally, bring students' attention back to the order they are now sitting in the circle—by color. Say, "Color is one way to organize the cards in your hand when you play this game." Demonstrate this by drawing seven cards and sorting them by color in your hand.

20. Students have been sitting for a while now; get them moving while remaining actively engaged by calling out one of the four shapes on the cards; students with that shape on their cards should go back to their chairs. Before they return to their seats, have them bring their card to you and retrieve whatever math organization tool you have selected, like a folder or a binder.

TEACHING TIP
Holding the Cards
Holding several cards at once can sometimes be challenging for little hands. Consider providing clips (clothespins work well) to help students hold the cards in place once they are fanned out.

TEACHING TIPS
Grouping Students
Predetermine the groups for this game, putting a student who exhibits leadership in each group. Groups of three seem to work well. Have each group get a deck of cards and sit together but not near another group. This lessens the chance of the decks becoming mixed up.

Emphasize Collaboration
For Part III, "Active Engagement," students should test the game out with their group, not playing against each other. The goal is for students to work together in understanding how to play the game and the math that is involved. When students have the opportunity to play the game independently (Part IV), they can play each other.

Running Out of Draw Cards
Some groups may run out of draw cards; in this case they need to shuffle all but the top card of the discard pile, stack the cards facedown as a draw pile, and continue play. Introduce this to groups as needed. During "The Link" part of the lesson, ask those students to do a whole-group share of what happened during their game and what they did so they could continue playing.

Part III: Active Engagement
Engage students to ensure they understand how to play the game.

21. Now give students the opportunity to explore the game in small groups. Each group should have a deck of cards. Distribute the directions for *Attributes Alike* (REPRODUCIBLE G-3) to each student. Students should place the directions in their binder, folder, or other math organization system you have designated. Task students with reading the directions to discover how the game of *Attributes Alike* is won.

22. As students are playing, circulate. Clarify misunderstandings and confirm correct play.

23. For the "Active Engagement" part of the lesson, place a time limit on the game, such as 20–30 minutes. This means that some groups will finish and begin another round, others will finish a round, while still others may not even complete a round if their cards are "unlucky."

Part IV: The Link
Students play the game independently.

24. Set students up for independent practice with the game. Designate a place in the classroom where the decks of cards can be stored and easily retrieved. Also determine how students will select whom and how many classmates they will play the game with. Let students know that they may play in twos, threes, or fours. Emphasize to students, "Be willing to play with different classmates each time you play."

MATH WORKSHOP AND SUMMARIZING THE EXPERIENCE

Teach this game at the beginning of the week to the whole class, then make it an integral part of your math workshop (for more on math workshop, see *Math Workshop* by Jennifer Lempp). Build in time to observe students playing the game. Note their individual skill level and the strategies being utilized; come together later in the week and hold a discussion. Revisit the defining attributes of the quadrilaterals used in this game—rectangle, square, trapezoid, and rhombus (they are closed figures, have four sides, and have vertices). Compare the defining attributes to some of the nondefining attributes like the ones used in this game (color and size).

Boxed In (A Game of Parallel and Perpendicular Moves)

Recommended Grade 4

Time Instruction: 30 minutes
Independent Play: 15–20 minutes

LEARNING TARGET
Post the game's Learning Target for students to see. This helps reinforce what students are responsible for learning as they play the game.

Grade 4:
- I can draw and identify lines that are parallel and perpendicular.

TIME SAVER
Reusable Game Boards
Instead of making consumable copies of the game board, laminate a set or place copies in plastic sleeves and provide dry erase markers to use during game play.

Overview
This game gives students practice with the concepts parallel and perpendicular, integral to many geometry standards. The game is similar to *Dots and Boxes*; however, players, in pairs, use a spinner to determine their next move. A spin determines one of three possible moves: parallel, perpendicular, or parallel and perpendicular. Players draw their line segment accordingly, connecting two dots on the game board. If a player closes a "box" (square) on their play, they claim the box by writing their first initial in it. The goal is to create and claim the most boxes on the game board.

Materials
- *Boxed In* Game Board (REPRODUCIBLE 4), 1 per pair of students
- *Boxed In* Spinner (REPRODUCIBLE 5), 1 per pair of students
- paper clips, 1 per pair of students
- pencils, 1 per pair of students
- *Boxed In* Game Directions (REPRODUCIBLE G-4), 1 per pair of students

Related Games
Game 6: Claim the Dots
(Classifying Angles and Lines)

Game 22: Sunshine (A Yahtzee-Like Game)

Key Questions

- What spin are you hoping for and why?
- Show an example of two parallel line segments on your game board.
- Show an example of two perpendicular line segments on your game board.
- What makes two lines parallel?
- What makes two lines perpendicular?

Teaching Directions

Part I: The Connection

Relate the game to students' ongoing work.

Ask students, "How many of you have been out to eat in a restaurant and receive a kids' menu featuring games you can play?" Continue, "The game we are going to play today may be familiar to you. On many kids' menus is a game called *Dots and Boxes*. It's a game where players connect the dots and try to be the first one to close the box. Today's game is called *Boxed In* and is played nearly the same way."

Part II: The Teaching

Introduce and model the game to students.

1. Gather students around a table or demonstration area in your classroom. Show students the *Boxed In* Game Board (REPRODUCIBLE 4). Make the connection again to real-life mathematics found on many kids' menus. Ask students, "What do you notice about the way the dots are arranged?" For those who have played the game before, ask, "What is different about this game board?" Point out the difference as needed: "This game board has a line segment predrawn in the middle—this is the starting line segment."

TECHNOLOGY TIP
Using an Interactive Whiteboard
If you use an interactive whiteboard in your classroom, scan in the *Boxed In* Game Board (REPRODUCIBLE 4) and open your ink layer so that you may interact with the board. Alternatively, in the whiteboard's toolkit, there is a geoboard that will suffice; just make sure you add the "start line segment" in the middle of the geoboard (as shown on REPRODUCIBLE 4). On a second page or using the split screen option, create a *Boxed In* Spinner (REPRODUCIBLE 5).

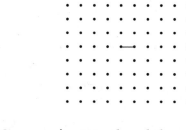

TEACHING TIP
Displaying the Game Board
One way to display the game board is outlined in the Technology Tip on the previous page. Alternatively, you may choose to project the game board using another device. Or you might simply copy the game board and have students gather around you (an option that works well is to have students arrange themselves in concentric circles, with one circle of students seated and one circle standing).

TEACHING TIP
Making Math Memorable
To help students remember the difference between parallel and perpendicular, use bodily kinesthetic memory techniques. For parallel, have students place both their arms straight out in front of them, parallel to the floor. Say the word *parallel* aloud as this is being done. Also point out that the spelling of *parallel* has two Ls side by side, just like the math symbol for parallel. For perpendicular, have students leave one arm parallel to the floor and bend their other arm up at the elbow so it forms a 90-degree angle. Touch the elbow of your bent arm to the straight arm while saying, "perpendicular" aloud.

2. Once you've introduced the game board, introduce the spinner (REPRODUCIBLE 5). Discuss the idea of equal chance and review the meanings of the terms *parallel* and *perpendicular*.

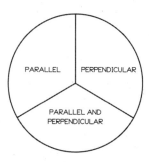

3. Tell students that the spinner dictates how they draw their line segment on the game board. Explain that you must draw your line segment as it relates to the previous line segment: "You must pay attention to the line segment your opponent draws because your line segment (move) must be either parallel or perpendicular to the line segment he drew on the game board. If you make a wrong move, you must erase the line and lose that turn."

4. Model how the game is played by playing a game—teacher versus the class. Spin the spinner and place a line segment on the game board that relates to the line segment already in the middle of the board.

5. Next, ask a student to spin the spinner, and explain to the students that this move must relate to the last line segment drawn on the game board (the previous move). For example, if the spinner lands on "parallel,"

the player must draw a line segment that is parallel to the last line segment drawn. If the spinner lands on the option marked "parallel and perpendicular," the player gets to draw two line segments accordingly.

6. Alternate play a few times, calling on various students to spin the spinner and make decisions about where to place the next line segment on the game board. This is an example of play after *perpendicular* and then *parallel* was spun:

Encourage students to think aloud; model this by thinking aloud about the various possibilities for where you could draw your line segment when it's your turn.

7. When a box is closed, demonstrate that the player writes his or her initial inside the box to "claim" it. As you are modeling the game, use a C for class and T for teacher.

8. A player loses a turn if the spin lands on an option that can no longer be taken on the game board. Play ends when both players have spun three consecutive times and cannot make a move, or when players have claimed all of the boxes. Model the game with the class until you feel students can play it independently in small groups.

9. Explain the scoring of the game to students: each player counts the number of boxes he claimed. The player with the highest number is declared the winner. Count the boxes to see who won—the teacher or the class?

 TEACHING TIP
Formative Assessment
Use a quick formative assessment technique like thumbs-up to assess whether students understand how to play the game. Say, "Thumbs up if you understand, thumbs down if you don't understand, and thumbs out if you sort of understand." If the majority of students don't have their thumbs up, continue guided teaching of the game.

Part III: Active Engagement

Engage students to ensure they understand how to play the game.

10. Now give students the opportunity to explore the game in pairs. Give each pair a game board and spinner.

11. As students are playing, circulate. Observe if they understand both the way the game is played (process) and the concept of parallel and perpendicular (content). Clarify misunderstandings and confirm correct play. Distribute the *Boxed In* Game Directions (REPRODUCIBLE G-4) to those who might need further support with the process. For those who need additional content support, try the "Making Math Memorable" Teaching Tip (page 20).

12. Students should finish a round of the game at approximately the same time. Task pairs who finish first with supporting other students.

Part IV: The Link

Students play the game independently.

13. Set students up for independent practice with the game. If students don't already have the directions, distribute the *Boxed In* Game Directions (REPRODUCIBLE G-4). Students should place the directions in their binder, folder, or other math organization system you have designated.

14. Designate and share a storage area for the *Boxed In* game boards (REPRODUCIBLE 4) and spinners (REPRODUCIBLE 5). This encourages students to be self-sufficient in gathering the materials whenever there is time allotted to independently play the game.

TEACHING TIPS

Providing Choice in Student Pairs

For this game, allow students to choose their partners or use a random strategy (such as pulling sticks with student names on them). If some students are not yet ready to play this game in pairs, team up two pairs to create a group of four to play.

Emphasize Collaboration

For Part III, "Active Engagement," students should test the game out with their partner, not playing against him or her. The goal is for students to work together in understanding *how* to play the game and the math that is involved. When students have the opportunity to play the game independently (Part IV), they can play each other.

MATH WORKSHOP AND SUMMARIZING THE EXPERIENCE

Teach this game at the beginning of the week to the whole class, then make it an integral part of your math workshop (for more on math workshop, see *Math Workshop* by Jennifer Lempp). Once students have had multiple opportunities to play *Boxed In*, have students create parallel and perpendicular representations using two popsicle sticks on their desk tops. Call out the terms and do a quick check of students' popsicles. Another idea is for students to create a work of art beginning with parallel and perpendicular lines using **REPRODUCIBLE 6, MY ART**. This is a similar to the Torrance Test of Creativity Thinking (TTCT) often used to help identify highly creative minds.

TEACHING TIP
Play It at Home!

The game *Boxed In* can be played easily at home. For home use, *Boxed In* needs only a copy of the game board, a copy of the spinner, a paper clip, and a pencil. Send home copies of the *Boxed In* Game Directions **(REPRODUCIBLE G-4)** as necessary.

ASSESSMENT

After students have had several experiences playing *Boxed In*, ask them to complete the assessment **(REPRODUCIBLE 7)** or journal in answer to the question, "What makes two lines parallel? What makes two lines perpendicular?"

Circle Up 360
(A Measurement Game Using Protractors)

Recommended Grade 4

Time Instruction: 20–30 minutes
Independent Play: 20–30 minutes

LEARNING TARGETS
Post the game's Learning Targets for students to see. This helps reinforce what students are responsible for learning as they play the game.

Grade 4:
- I know that angles are formed when two rays share a common end point.
- I know an angle is measured with reference to a circle with its center at the common end point of the two rays.
- I can measure angles using a protractor.

TEACHING TIPS
Reusable Templates
Instead of using paper plates or making consumable copies of the *Circle UP 360* Paper Plate Template, laminate a set or place copies in plastic sleeves and provide dry erase markers to use during game play.

Quiet Dice
Rolling dice can create lots of noise. To lessen the noise, use foam dice or pad students' workspaces with foam or fabric placemats.

Overview
This game gives students practice constructing and measuring angles. Each player has their own "game board"—a paper plate. Players take turns drawing and labeling angles on their plates. After players have drawn six angles on each of their plates, they measure the remaining angle on each of their plates. The goal is to be the player with the smallest remaining angle on their plate.

Materials
- tape, 3 18-inch strips per group of 4 students
- protractors, 1 per student
- paper plates or *Circle Up 360* Paper Plate Template (REPRODUCIBLE 8), 1 per student
- dice (labeled *1–6*), 2 per pair of students
- *Circle Up 360* Game Directions (REPRODUCIBLE G-5), 1 per student

Related Game
Game 6: Claim the Dots

Key Questions
- How did you choose which rolled number should be the tens and which should be the ones for your angle?
- What types of angles have you used in this game? (acute)
- What is the definition of or how would you describe an acute, right, and obtuse angle?

Teaching Directions

Part I: The Connection

Relate the game to students' ongoing work.

Ask students, "Have you ever done or seen someone do a 360? In what sports or activities have you performed a 360 or seen someone do one?" Responses might include pivoting in basketball, skateboarding, ice skating, doing turns in ballet, or spinning on a merry-go-round. Once students have offered real-life connections, tell them a complete circle has 360 degrees. Talk about the properties of a circle and, in particular, the center point of a circle.

Part II: The Teaching

Introduce and model the game to students.

1. Prepare a desk or table for modeling the game. Place strips of tape across the surface to form intersecting lines and angles similar to this:

2. Gather students around the demonstration area. Model how to use the protractor, measuring the angles created by the tape lines.

3. Now give each student a protractor. Arrange students into groups of four and have each group designate their own demonstration area (a desk or table) and gather around it.

4. Give each group three pieces of tape and have them stick the tape to the surface of their demonstration area to form intersecting lines and angles.

5. Task each student with measuring the angles created by the intersecting tape lines.

TEACHING TIP

Reviewing and Demonstrating 360 Degrees

Use four pieces of 12-by-9–inch construction paper of four various colors so students can easily see the demonstration. Place the four pieces of paper so that all four share the same point (see sample). Review that each angle of the rectangle is 90 degrees (90 + 90 + 90 + 90 = 360 or 4 × 90 = 360). Round off the corners to form a circle demonstrating 360 degrees.

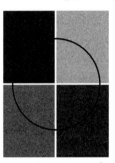

TECHNOLOGY TIP

Using Online Video

To support the discussion around 360s, show students online videos of people (from amateurs to Olympians!) performing 360s.

TEACHING TIPS

Arranging Students

For the demonstration area, have students make two concentric circles. In the first circle, students kneel or sit; in the second, students stand. This ensures that everyone can see what's happening.

Working in Groups Rather Than Individually

Because all students are measuring the same angles, having them work within small groups can minimize errors while also promoting talk around the mathematics, further solidifying their understanding.

6. When you feel students are comfortable using a protractor, gather them once again around the main demonstration area. Bring students' attention to the "Learning Targets" (see page 24), in particular the target that addresses angles as they relate to circles. Say, "An angle is measured with reference to a circle with its center at the common endpoint of the rays." Point to the corresponding part of the protractor:

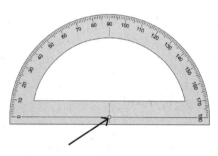

7. Continue, "The shape of a protractor is half a circle or a semicircle. Each of the marks on the semicircle measures the two rays with a common endpoint or angle."

8. Next explain that students are going to play a game involving these concepts. Show students the *Circle Up 360* Paper Plate Template (REPRODUCIBLE 8) or construct your own template by drawing the starting ray on a paper plate.

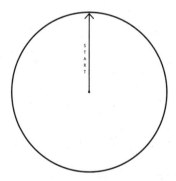

TECHNOLOGY TIP
Using an Interactive Whiteboard
If an interactive whiteboard is in the classroom, use the tools to create a large circle to demonstrate the game. On that same page, place two interactive dice and a protractor; both can be found in the whiteboard's toolkit.

9. Explain that each student will have a paper plate (or paper plate template) and be tasked with drawing angles on their plate. To determine the angle that they will need to construct, they will roll two dice.

10. Ask a student to roll the two dice and announce the numbers rolled. Explain that the two numbers need to be used to create one two-digit number, with either roll being used in the tens or ones place. For example, if a 1 and a 5 are rolled, the two-digit number (angle) could be 15 or 51. It's up to the player to decide which number to use to draw her angle.

11. For purposes of modeling the game, have the class decide the number (angle) together. Then demonstrate how to draw the corresponding angle on the paper plate using a protractor. Point out that the starting ray has already been drawn and students will need to work clockwise around the circle. When drawing the angle, take the ray all the way to the circle edge. This will help students read the angle since the rays will extend out through the protractor where the numbers and hash marks are.

12. Once the angle is drawn, explain that the other player must then measure the accuracy of his opponent's angle. If it is correct, write the angle's measurement on the plate, inside of the corresponding angle. Emphasize the importance of this step because it will aid students in measuring angles correctly.

13. Repeat Steps 10–12, pointing out that the previous ray drawn is the new starting ray. Tell and show, "The previous ray drawn becomes part of the next angle."

14. Now introduce the objective of game: "The winner of the game is the player with the smallest remaining angle on her plate after six turns (angles)."

15. Continue modeling how the game is played, rolling the dice, constructing angles, and then checking their measurements. Give various students the opportunity to roll the dice and invite the class to support each student in determining the measurement of the next angle.

TEACHING TIP
Discussing Strategy
While accurately measuring angles is the goal of this game, students may soon discover that strategy and probability skills will be helpful in winning (of course, luck also plays a role). Resist discussing this when modeling the game; rather, bring it up once students have had several opportunities to play the game (see Part IV, "The Link").

16. Play a full six rounds so that only one angle remains on the game board. As an example, this is a game board from a fourth-grade classroom, after six rounds:

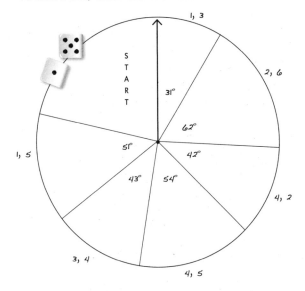

TEACHING TIP
Grouping Students
Be thoughtful in how you group students for this game. If students are more experienced and have demonstrated accuracy in measuring angles with a protractor, have them play in pairs. If, on the other hand, students are struggling or lack experience with a protractor, have them play in teams of two (groups of four). This gives students the opportunity to mentor and support each other.

Part III: Active Engagement
Engage students to ensure they understand how to play the game.

17. Now give students the opportunity to explore the game with each other. Decide whether to have students play in pairs or teams of two (see Teaching Tip, "Grouping Students").

18. Each pair or group will need a protractor, pencil, and two dice labeled *1–6*. If students are playing in pairs, each student also needs a paper plate or template. If playing in teams of two, each team needs a paper plate or template.

TEACHING TIP
Defining Accuracy
Remind students that it's important that each player or team measure their own angle as well as their opponent's angle for accuracy before recording any measurements. Precision is important; in the real world, being off by a degree can be detrimental to an architect. However, in the classroom, since the tools are pencils and paper (not computers, lumber, and steel), precision can be broader. Typically, most teachers define accuracy as being within one to two degrees.

19. As students are playing, circulate. Watch them measure. Provide additional support when necessary on how to place the protractor, read it, and record the angle measurement. Ensure that students are taking turns in constructing and measuring each other's angles.

Part IV: The Link

Students play the game independently.

20. Set students up for independent practice with the game. Distribute the directions for *Circle Up 360* (REPRODUCIBLE G-5). Students should place the directions in their binders, folders, or other math organization system you have designated.

21. Designate and share a storage space for all the materials used in *Circle Up 360*. This encourages students to be self-sufficient in gathering the materials whenever there is time allotted to independently play the game.

DIFFERENTIATING YOUR INSTRUCTION

Students Play as One Team

One way to change up how the game is played is to have students play as one team on one game board (paper plate). Players alternate who draws the angle and who checks for accuracy. This takes the focus off of someone being "the winner" and encourages students to work collaboratively, which often leads to deeper mathematical discussions. This is also a way to shorten the duration of time needed to play the game.

MATH WORKSHOP AND SUMMARIZING THE EXPERIENCE

Teach this game at the beginning of the week to the whole class, then make it an integral part of your math workshop (for more on math workshop, see *Math Workshop* by Jennifer Lempp). Have students write their names on the backs of the paper plates and turn the plates in every time they finish a game. At the end of the week, after all students have had a chance to play the game, distribute the paper plates randomly and have students practice measuring the seven angles (six rounds plus the angle that remains at the end). What do all seven angles add up to (360 degrees)? Also have students post their scores on a Class Records Chart. Each time a new record is set, students post their "lowest angle measurement" and place their initials next to it. This helps keep students both motivated and on task.

Claim the Dots
(Classifying Angles and Lines)

Recommended Grade 4

Time Instruction: 45–60 minutes
Independent Play: 20–30 minutes

TEACHING TIPS
Transparent Chips
Transparent chips work best for this game as you can still see the game board through the chip. However, if transparent chips are not available, any chip will do; you can also substitute chips with cubes or tiles of two different colors.

Reusable Game Boards
Instead of making consumable copies of the game board, consider laminating a set or placing copies in plastic sleeves.

TIME SAVER
Managing Materials
Save time by organizing the transparent chips into sets prior to the lesson. Each set should contain 24 same-color chips, with there being enough different-color sets for everyone to play (each pair of students must play with two different-color sets). Place two sets (each a different color—48 chips total) in quart-size sandwich bags and include one die. Bundle this with the *Claim the Dots* Game Board (**REPRODUCIBLE 9**) and *Claim the Dots* Game Directions (**REPRODUCIBLE G-6**). Sometimes you might make additional copies of the directions and post them throughout the classroom for students to refer to during independent play.

Overview
In this game, students practice identifying and classifying angles and lines, working toward mastering similar standards. Students roll a die and use the game's legend to translate the number to an angle or lines. They then place a transparent chip on the matching angle or lines on the game board. Once a chip has been placed, it can be secured with another of the same player's chips should they again roll the same angle or lines. If a player's chip is not secured with a second chip, their opponent can knock their chip off the game board should they roll the same angle or lines. Ultimately, the player with the most dots "claimed" wins the game.

Materials
- *Claim the Dots* Game Board (**REPRODUCIBLE 9**), 1 per pair of students
- dice (labeled *1–6*), 1 per pair of students
- transparent chips, 2 sets of 24, each set a different color, per pair of students
- *Claim the Dots* Game Directions (**REPRODUCIBLE G-6**), 1 per pair of students

Related Games
Game 4: Boxed In (A Game of Parallel and Perpendicular Moves)

Game 22: Sunshine (A Yahtzee-Like Game)

Key Questions

- What is the difference between parallel lines and perpendicular lines?
- How are perpendicular lines and intersecting lines similar?
- What makes an angle acute?
- What makes an angle obtuse?
- How many degrees are in a right angle?

Teaching Directions

Part I: The Connection

Relate the game to students' ongoing work.

Take students on a short walk outside your school building with the mission to observe angles and lines in their surroundings. For example, point out that the school crossing sign has three acute angles that create an equilateral triangle. Look for parallel lines in the parking lot or at the curbs. Note that the flag pole is perpendicular to the ground. Show how bike racks have two metal parallel lines that are perpendicular with the top and bottom of the rack.

Part II: The Teaching

Introduce and model the game to students.

1. Group students in pairs and give each pair a *Claim the Dots* Game Board (REPRODUCIBLE 9) and two sets of 24 transparent discs each (each set needs to be a different color).

2. After students are paired up and seated with their game boards and chips, explain that they will be learning as a class how to play the game *Claim the Dots*. Just as the game title sounds, the objective is to claim as many dots as possible on the game board.

LEARNING TARGETS
Post the game's Learning Targets for students to see. This helps reinforce what students are responsible for learning as they play the game.

Grade 4:
- I can draw and identify angles and lines.
- I can classify shapes by properties of their angles and lines.

TEACHING TIP
Brain Compatible Instruction
Brain researchers highly support movement while learning. Movement helps tap into the episodic memory pathway, enhancing retention. Simply getting up and walking about helps activate the mind in addition to providing opportunities for connections.

TEACHING TIP
Pairing Students Intentionally

For both Part II and Part III, there are a number of ways to group students for this lesson and others in this book or across disciplines. To keep the lesson flow moving, using preassigned teacher pairings is both a time-saver and helps ensure quality practice of the Learning Targets. Two teacher-assigned pairings work well with this lesson. The first is pairing students to mix skill levels. Students learn well when different skills and levels are mixed, ensuring varying abilities are intermingled. Another is pairing for classroom management. Preassign partners to make sure students who need to be separated are kept apart and keep all on task.

TIME SAVER
Preparing the Legend

The legend is critical to playing this game; to ensure everyone has access to it, consider displaying it poster-size so everyone can see it. Alternatively, clearly write it on the board. Another idea is to have the *Claim the Dots* Game Directions (**REPRODUCIBLE G-6**) available for each pair of students so they can easily refer to the legend as well as preview the directions.

TECHNOLOGY TIP
Using an Interactive Whiteboard

Another way to introduce the game to your class is through the use of an interactive whiteboard. Interactive whiteboards offer interactive dice; students can be asked to tap the whiteboard to roll the die, and everyone can more easily see the roll.

3. Next, share the game's legend:

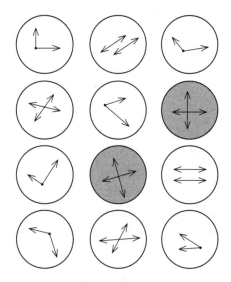

Explain that part of playing the game is rolling the die and using the legend to "translate" the number rolled into a line or angle that you will then look for on the game board. For example, if a 3 is rolled, per the legend, you will need to find an obtuse angle on the game board.

4. Using the legend, review the concepts acute angle, right angle, obtuse angle, intersecting lines, perpendicular lines, and parallel lines. Point out that the *Claim the Dots* Game Board (**REPRODUCIBLE 9**) has two of each type of line or angle. Roll a die and call out the number rolled. Ask students to find one or both of the correct representations on their game boards. For example, if a 5 is rolled, per the legend, students would find the two dots containing perpendicular lines on their game board:

5. Once you feel students are comfortable with the angles and lines they are being asked to identify, explain that like most games,

play alternates in this one. Ask each pair of students to determine a Player 1 and Player 2 and decide their playing chips (each player needs a different-color set of chips).

6. Roll the die and announce to the class what number has been rolled.

7. Instruct all Player 1s to look at their game board and find the dot with the corresponding angle or lines. They should then place one of their colored chips on it.

8. Roll the die again. This time ask all Player 2s to find the corresponding angle or lines and place a chip from their set on it.

9. Soon the opportunity to knock an opponent's chip off the board and claim the dot will occur. Explain, "If your opponent rolls a number that you have already rolled, they can knock your chip off the game board and place their chip on the dot instead."

10. Tell students, "To secure a dot, a player needs to place two of their chips on the same dot. You can do this when you roll a number you have already rolled. When a chip has a second same-color chip on top of it, the chips can no longer be knocked off the board and the dot is "claimed" by that player.

11. Roll the die as a class a few times, having players take turns until students have a feel for how the game is played. Depending on the time duration allowed for the game, it is likely that a player will roll a number for a dot that is already claimed with two chips. In this case, that player loses a turn.

Part III: Active Engagement
Engage students to ensure they understand how to play the game.

12. Now give each pair of students a die and have them continue exploring the game, only they now alternate rolling the die with their partner. If the *Claim the Dots* Game Directions

TEACHING TIP
Formative Assessment
Use a quick formative assessment technique like thumbs-up to determine if students understand the game. Say, "Thumbs up if you understand, thumbs down if you don't understand, and thumbs out if you sort of understand." If the majority of the class does not give you a thumbs-up, continue guided teaching of the game.

TEACHING TIP

The Importance of Asking Questions
Asking key questions assists you in understanding how or if students are developing strategies. As students answer key questions, students get to hear other students' thinking and further develop their own understanding of the content.

(REPRODUCIBLE G-6) has not been previously distributed, this would be the time to do so.

13. As students are playing, circulate. Are they understanding the content being practiced? Check in by asking key questions like, "Which angle on the board is acute, and how do you know?" or "Show me a set of lines that are both intersecting lines and perpendicular." (See Key Questions, page 31.)

14. To wrap up Part III, ask students to finish the turn they are currently on. Then have each player count the number of dots they claimed (those dots that have two of their colored chips on them). Explain that each claimed dot equates to a game point. Which player has the most claimed dots?

Part IV: The Link
Students play the game independently.

15. Set students up for independent practice with the game. Designate and share a storage space for all the materials used in *Claim the Dots*. This encourages students to be self-sufficient in gathering the materials whenever there is time allotted to independently play the game.

MATH WORKSHOP AND SUMMARIZING THE EXPERIENCE
Teach this game at the beginning of the week to the whole class, then make it an integral part of your math workshop (for more on math workshop, see *Math Workshop* by Jennifer Lempp). Come together as a class later in the week and review the types of angles and lines identified in the game. See if students can classify two-dimensional figures based on the presence or absence of parallel or perpendicular lines, or the presence or absence of angles of a specified size. The polygon cards **(REPRODUCIBLE 10)** for Game 7 *Compare* (Geometry Version) could be used for this review, using the Key Questions at the beginning of this lesson.

TECHNOLOGY TIP
Using an Interactive Whiteboard
If an interactive whiteboard is available, prepare a page with a variety of polygons. Have students sort them into shapes with parallel lines or perpendicular lines and identify where those are to their classmates.

Compare (Geometry Version)

Overview

In this game, students compare and analyze shapes using a special deck of polygon cards. The player who has a card featuring a polygon with more sides than the one it's being compared with wins the hand. This game serves as a springboard to introducing polygon names and terminology like sides and vertices.

Materials

- *Compare (Geometry Version)* Polygon Cards (REPRODUCIBLE 10), 1 deck per pair of students
- *Compare (Geometry Version)* Game Directions (REPRODUCIBLE G-7), 1 per pair of students

Related Games

Game 3: Attributes Alike

Game 14: Geometry Go Fish

Key Questions

- Do you know the number of sides a shape has just by glancing at it? Show me a card whose polygon you can do this with.
- What is the name of that polygon/shape?

Recommended Grades K–1

Time Instruction: 30 minutes
Independent Play: 15–20 minutes

LEARNING TARGETS
Post the game's Learning Targets for students to see. This helps reinforce what students are responsible for learning as they play the game.

Grade K:
- I can correctly name shapes.
- I can identify two-dimensional shapes.
- I can compare similarities and differences of two-dimensional shapes.

Grade 1:
- I can describe shapes using defining attributes.

TIME SAVERS
A Deck of Cards
For the purpose of this game, a deck of cards is two copies of each page of the five-page reproducible. This means a deck will have 54 cards.

Reusable Cards
To ensure the longevity of cards, use thick paper stock and/or laminate them. Store each deck in a sandwich bag.

Color-Coding Decks
To keep decks of cards from getting mixed up with other sets, use a different color of paper for each deck.

TECHNOLOGY TIP
Using an Interactive Whiteboard
If you use an interactive whiteboard, you can pull the shapes up on the whiteboard rather than using the cards. To do this, after opening the mathematics tools, search for 2-D geometric shapes. Using just the polygons, select a triangle, rectangle, pentagon, and hexagon and place them at the bottom of a notebook page. Have students drag two of the polygons up. Continue with Steps 3–5. On a second page, show two polygons that have the same number of sides, like a rectangle and trapezoid. Use this page to continue with Step 6.

TEACHING TIP
Displaying the Shapes
There are several options besides using cards from the deck to model this game; consider an option that best allows everyone in the class to see what's happening. Use an interactive whiteboard (see the Technology Tip above) or enlarge five of the cards from a deck of Polygon Cards or simply draw your own polygons on five pieces of large construction paper (the shapes you'll need are a triangle, rectangle, pentagon, hexagon, and rhombus or trapezoid).

Teaching Directions
Part I: The Connection
Relate the game to students' ongoing work.

Gather students around a table in two concentric circles (one seated and one standing) or seat them on the floor. If students have played the game *Compare (Shake and Spill)*—Game 8 in the companion book *Math Games for Number and Operations and Algebraic Thinking*—reenact a few rounds of play by having a student shake and spill ten two-color counters (in this case, the two colors are yellow and red). After the counters spill, ask students, "Are there more red counters, more yellow, or is it the same amount of both red and yellow?" Tell students that today they'll be learning yet another game that entails comparing. In this game they will be using cards with pictures of polygons on them. Explain, "You will be comparing the number of sides of the polygons."

Part II: The Teaching
Introduce and model the game to students.

1. Pull the following four cards from a deck of Polygon Cards (REPRODUCIBLE 10): a triangle, rectangle, pentagon, and hexagon.

2. Ask a student to select one of the four cards and another student to select another.

3. Ask students, "What do you notice about the polygons on the cards you selected?" Students may point out that one polygon has more sides, corners, or is larger than the other. Students may also be eager to name the shapes.

4. Emphasize to students that in this game, they specifically compare the number of sides of

the polygons. Ask, "How many sides does each polygon on the selected cards have?"

5. Now introduce the objective of the game: "Whoever has the card featuring the polygon with the most sides earns both cards for this round."

6. Sometimes in the game, cards might be drawn that feature polygons with the same number of sides. Demonstrate what to do if this happens by asking one student to select the card with a rectangle on it and introducing another card featuring a shape with the same sides as a rectangle, such as a rhombus.

7. Ask all of the students, "What do you notice about the polygons on these two selected cards?" The game is designed so that students not only become more familiar with differences in shapes, but also similarities.

8. Once a student has shared that both polygons have the same number of sides, introduce yet another part of the game: if the two selected cards feature polygons with the same number of sides, the cards stay in play.

9. Next show students an entire deck of Polygon Cards. Tell them there are 54 cards in the deck. Emphasize that at the beginning of each game, it is important to shuffle the cards first. Demonstrate to students how one might shuffle the deck. Then deal the cards to two players. Instruct students to not touch the cards until you have finished dealing. Once the cards have been dealt out equally, players should stack their cards into a pile, facedown, in front of them.

 TEACHING TIP
Shuffling Cards
Younger students are typically not able to shuffle the cards. If this is the case, demonstrate how to mix the cards with your hands, being careful to keep all the cards facing down. Then gather the cards into two neat stacks. Students also have the option of leaving the cards spread out (instead of stacking them), especially if their playing area isn't large enough.

10. Play a few rounds of the game as a whole class, now using the deck of cards. Both players draw the top card from their stacks and turn it over. Players compare the two cards: which card features the polygon with the most sides? The player who has that card takes both of the cards and sets them aside—that player has "earned" both cards.

11. If the polygons on both cards have the same number of sides, the cards remain where they are and players each draw the next top card from their stacks, this time placing the card faceup on top of the previous card. The player who has the card featuring the polygon with the most sides now takes both the cards from the previous play and the current cards and sets them aside (so the player earns four cards).

12. Once all the cards in both stacks have been played, players count the cards they've earned. The player with the most cards wins.

13. Have players total their two numbers; the two numbers should always add up to 54 because there are 54 cards in each deck.

Part III: Active Engagement
Engage students to ensure they understand how to play the game.

14. Now give students the opportunity to play the game in pairs. Each pair of students will need a deck of Polygon Cards. They may also need a copy of the *Compare (Geometry Version)* Game Directions (REPRODUCIBLE G-7).

15. As students are playing, circulate. Observe; are students counting the number of sides of the polygons and comparing? To confirm that students are actively comparing, listen for vocabulary like more, greater, less, and equal to.

16. Pairs should finish at approximately the same time. For those pairs of students who finish first, task them with shuffling, dealing, and stacking their cards again.

TEACHING TIP
Pairing Students
When pairing students for this game, pair students of similar ability levels. Each pair should have like abilities in understanding the relationship between numbers and quantities and connecting counting to cardinality.

Part IV: The Link

Students play the game independently.

17. Set students up for independent practice of the game. Designate a place in the classroom where the decks of cards can be stored and easily retrieved. If students don't already have the directions, distribute the *Compare (Geometry Version)* Game Directions (REPRO-DUCIBLE G-7) and have students place the directions in their binder, folder, or other math organization system you have designated.

18. Discuss the importance of keeping the cards together and not mixing up the decks. Suggest and then model how students should work in pairs far enough away from another pair of students so that the decks do not get mixed together (having each deck copied on a different color of paper helps as well).

DIFFERENTIATING YOUR INSTRUCTION

Scoring Points Versus Cards

For students needing an additional challenge, change up the way the game is scored. In this version, students compare cards and the player whose card features the polygon with the most sides earns the difference in the number of sides rather than the two cards. For example, if a triangle and an octagon are being compared, the player with the octagon earns five points because the difference in the sides between the two shapes is five. Students will need paper and pencil to keep track of the scoring. This variation not only increases the engagement for those students needing more challenge but adds another layer of luck and skill.

MATH WORKSHOP AND SUMMARIZING THE EXPERIENCE

Teach this game at the beginning of the week to the whole class, then make it an integral part of your math workshop (for more on math workshop, see *Math Workshop* by Jennifer Lempp). Come together later in the week and hold a discussion. Review the vocabulary students have been using (such as sides and vertices) and add the words to a word wall. Then post four large pieces of chart paper around the room and title them as follows:

    3-Sided Polygons

    4-Sided Polygons

    5-Sided Polygons

    6-Sided Polygons

Have students do a gallery walk and draw polygons on each poster. Review the drawings as a whole class. Does each drawing correspond with the title of the poster it's on? Label each polygon if it has a special name like so many of the quadrilaterals do—rectangle, square, rhombus, trapezoid, etc. This activity moves students toward reasoning with shapes and their attributes.

Compare (Measurement Version)

Recommended Grades K–2

Time   Instruction: 45–60 minutes

Independent Play: 20–30 minutes

TEACHING TIP
A Deck of Cards

In this game players can use numeral cards or regular playing cards. If using numeral cards, the companion book *Math Games for Number and Operations in Algebraic Thinking* offers a reproducible for making numeral cards (see **REPRODUCIBLE B**). For the purpose of this game, a deck of cards is Ace–10 of each of the four suits if using playing cards or four copies of each number 1–10 if using numeral cards. Remove all face cards, jokers, and wild cards. Aces remain, serving as the number 1. When complete, a deck should have 40 cards.

TIME SAVERS
Coding Cards

Whether using numeral cards or a deck of playing cards, code each set to keep it complete. Do this by placing a small symbol in the corner of each set's card; use a different symbol for each set so that if the sets become mixed up, they can be easily sorted.

Organizing Interlocking Cubes

For the purpose of this game, organize sets of approximately 100 cubes in tubs or containers that students can reach into easily with their hands. Tubs should be placed in the middle of the playing space so all players can easily access cubes.

Overview

In this version of *Compare*, students practice building and ordering cube sticks by length and then comparing the lengths. Players start the game by dealing a customized deck of numeral cards (1–10) or playing cards (Ace–10). Each player turns over the top card and uses interlocking cubes to build a stick of cubes corresponding to the number on their card. Next, players order and compare the lengths of their cube sticks. Each player earns points based on the difference in the number of cubes between their stick and the next shortest stick. Ultimately, the player who earns the most points (cubes) wins.

While this lesson is written to address Learning Targets common for first grade, it can also be used to address kindergarten and second-grade Learning Targets.

Materials

- numeral cards (1–10) or playing cards (Ace–10), 1 deck per group of 2–4 students

- interlocking cubes, approximately 100 per group of 2–4 students

- *Compare (Measurement Version)* Game Directions (REPRODUCIBLE G-8), 1 per group of 2–4 students

Related Game

Game 7: Compare (Geometry Version)

Key Questions

- Can you order the sticks of cubes from shortest to longest? Please demonstrate.

- Can you order the sticks of cubes from longest to shortest? Please demonstrate.

- How much longer is Player 1's stick of cubes than Player 2's stick?

Teaching Directions

Part I: The Connection

Relate the game to students' ongoing work.

Ask students, "How many of you have heard the expression, 'That person got the short end of the stick'?" Explain the expression's meaning: the person got the bad end of a bargain, contest, or situation. Relate a story that likely happens at every school, like the lunchroom running out of an item. Say, "If the school cafeteria ran out of pizza and the remaining students had to have a sandwich instead, you might say they got the short end of the stick." Explain that today students will be playing a game where "getting the short end of the stick" may not be all that bad.

Part II: The Teaching

Introduce and model the game to students.

1. Gather students around a table in two concentric circles (one seated and one standing) or seat them on the floor. Place a prepared deck of cards (see "Materials" list) as well as a tub of approximately 100 interlocking cubes in the demonstration area.

2. Tell students they will be playing the measurement version of a game called *Compare*. Select two volunteers to help model the game with you; have them move next to you.

3. Shuffle the card deck and deal 13 cards to each player (since there are three players, one card in the deck will be left over). Instruct students to not touch the cards until you are

LEARNING TARGETS

Post the game's Learning Targets for students to see. This helps reinforce what students are responsible for learning as they play the game.

Grade K:
- I can compare two sticks of cubes to see which has more or less.
- I can determine the difference in cubes of the two sticks.

Grade 1:
- I can order three sticks of cubes by length.
- I can compare the lengths of three sticks of cubes and determine the difference.

Grade 2:
- I can use a ruler to measure how much longer one stick of cubes is than another.

TEACHING TIP
Shuffling Cards
Younger students are typically not able to shuffle the cards. If this is the case, demonstrate how to mix the cards with your hands, being careful to keep all the cards facing down.

done dealing. Once the cards have been dealt out equally, players stack their cards into a pile, facedown, in front of them.

4. Ask each player to draw the top card from their stack and place it faceup next to their stack.

5. Say, "The number on the card tells you how many interlocking cubes you are to take and snap together." If you are using regular playing cards, point out that the Ace cards serve as the number 1.

6. Each player snaps together a stick of cubes corresponding to their card. For example:

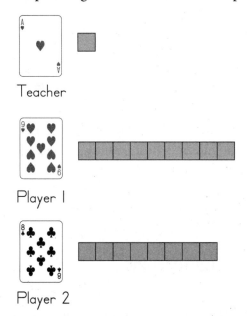

7. Once each player has built a stick of cubes to match the corresponding number on their cards, instruct students to place the sticks in order from shortest to longest to compare the lengths. Using the above example, the sticks would be ordered like this:

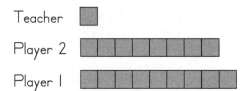

8. Now explain that each player earns points based on the difference in the number of

cubes between their stick and the next shortest stick. Return to the sticks of cubes currently in play. Walk students through the scoring for this round, beginning with the two longest sticks. For example, Player 1 has a stick of 9 cubes and Player 2 has a stick of 8 cubes; therefore, Player 1 keeps one cube because their stick was one cube longer (the difference between 8 and 9). Break Player 1's remaining cubes apart and place them back in the tub.

9. Now move to the remaining two sticks; compare their lengths and score accordingly. Player 2 had a stick of 8 and the teacher had only 1 cube, so Player 2 keeps the difference of 7 cubes. Player 2's one remaining cube goes back in the tub.

10. Now only one player is left to score—the player with the shortest stick. Explain that the player with the shortest stick always keeps all the cubes in their stick. In this round this means the teacher only gets to keep 1 cube, but depending on the round, having the shortest stick can mean keeping a lot more cubes.

11. Continue to play several more rounds as a class.

12. Be sure to model what to do in the event of a tie, meaning two or more sticks of equal cubes are created. For example, the teacher has a stick of 6 cubes, Player 2 has 4 cubes, and Player 3 has 6 cubes. Their sticks are arranged in order as follows:

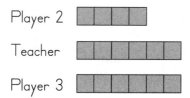

13. Explain that the two players with sticks of 6 cubes have the longest sticks, which are 2

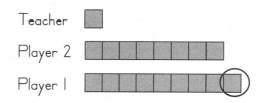

Player 1 keeps one cube because their stick is one cube longer than the next longest stick.

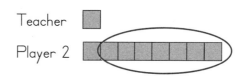

Player 2 keeps seven cubes because their stick is seven cubes longer than the shortest stick.

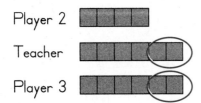

Player 2

Teacher

Player 3

The teacher and Player 3 each keep two cubes because their sticks are two cubes longer than the shortest stick.

cubes longer than the shorter stick of 4 cubes. Those players would each keep the difference, which is 2 cubes. The player with the shortest stick, in this scenario Player 2 with a stick of 4, keeps all 4 of her cubes. In this example, the "short end of the stick" got the better deal.

14. Next tell students that while it is possible yet unlikely, there may be a time when every player has the same length of sticks (meaning they all drew the same card number). When this happens, to settle the tie, all players go back to their stack of cards and draw the next top card. They add that number onto their stick of cubes, and then recompare sticks. If it happens to be the last round, meaning there are no more cards to play, then the game ends.

15. Finally, explain how to determine which player wins. Say, "When all of the cards are played, the game is over. To find out who is the winner, all players add up their total number of earned cubes into one stick, and the player with the longest stick wins."

Part III: Active Engagement
Engage students to ensure they understand how to play the game.

16. Now give students the opportunity to play the game in small groups. Give each group a deck of cards (see "Materials" list for instructions on preparing the decks) and a tub of approximately 100 interlocking cubes. Students may also need a copy of the *Compare (Measurement Version)* Game Directions (**REPRODUCIBLE G-8**). Encourage groups to spread out around the classroom so that the decks of cards don't get mixed up.

17. As students are playing, circulate. Ask key question such as, "Show me the order of the sticks of cubes from shortest to longest." Or, "How much longer is Player One's stick than Player Two's?" (See Key Questions, page 41.)

TEACHING TIP
Grouping Students
Though the game can be played with varying group sizes, grouping students in threes for Part III might work best, as this is the group size used for modeling the game. Should the numbers not work out just right, students could also play in teams; this way reluctant learners or students who need additional time in learning procedures of new activities have a partner.

Since this game involves the "luck of the cards," randomly grouping students into threes will suffice. You may have students self-select their groups, number off, or use a classroom management technique like pulling sticks labeled with students' names.

18. After students have had a chance to play at least one complete game, instruct groups to break apart any cubes that are still interlocked and place them back into the appropriate tubs as well as put each deck of cards back together.

Part IV: The Link

Students play the game independently.

19. Set up students for independent practice of the game. Designate a place in the classroom where the decks of cards and tubs of cubes can be stored and easily retrieved. If students don't already have the directions, distribute the *Compare (Measurement Version)* Game Directions (REPRODUCIBLE G-8) and have students place the directions in their binder, folder, or other math organization system you have designated. Alternatively, enlarge and display the game directions in a predetermined place in the classroom.

MATH WORKSHOP AND SUMMARIZING THE EXPERIENCE

Teach this game at the beginning of the week to the whole class, then make it an integral part of your math workshop (for more on math workshops, see *Math Workshop* by Jennifer Lempp). After students have had ample time to play the game, bring them back together for a whole-class activity. Pass out a card to each student. Have them build the number using snap cubes. Then have students stand with their cube sticks and put on some music. Tell students, "Walk randomly around the classroom. When the music stops, the classmate(s) nearest to you is your Compare partner or group. Whose stick is the shortest? Let's try to keep groups to sizes of two to four classmates while not leaving anyone out." Most students love music, moving, and socializing with classmates. This culminating activity provides these opportunities while channeling the talk toward the Learning Targets.

DIFFERENTIATING YOUR INSTRUCTION

Struggling Learners

To further help those who may be struggling with the procedures of the game, rearrange students so each group has a student who has mastered the game directions and can reteach the game as needed.

Groups of Four

Playing this game in groups of four can add to the complexity of the game. There is more opportunity for players to draw the same cards, and therefore create the same lengths of cube sticks. This will especially add a layer of difficulty to the game when players determine the number of cubes each earns.

ASSESSMENT

After students have had several experiences playing the game *Compare*, ask them to complete the assessment (REPRODUCIBLE 11).

Connect Four (A Graphing Game)

Recommended Grade 5

Time Instruction: 30–45 minutes
Independent Play: 20–30 minutes

TEACHING TIPS
Don't Have Colored Counters?
As an alternative to using colored counters, laminate the game board or place it in a plastic sleeve. Have students use two different colors of dry erase markers to mark the game board. Yet another option, substitute counters for two different coins like pennies and nickels.

Quiet Dice
Rolling dice can create lots of noise. To lessen the noise, use foam dice or pad students' workspaces with foam or fabric placemats.

TIME SAVER
Managing Materials
Save time by organizing the counters into sets prior to the lesson. Place each set in a quart-size sandwich bag and include one die. Bundle this with the *Connect Four* Game Board **(REPRODUCIBLE 12)** and *Connect Four* Game Directions **(REPRODUCIBLE G-9)**. Consider also making additional copies of the directions and posting them throughout the classroom for students to refer to during independent play.

Overview
In this game, students practice graphing points on a coordinate plane. Players roll a die twice; the first roll determines the number for the *x*-coordinate and the second roll determines the number for the *y*-coordinate. Players place a colored counter at the corresponding intersection of the plane (game board). The objective is to be the first player to connect four colored counters in a row (diagonally, horizontally, or vertically).

Materials
- dice (labeled *1–6*), 1 per pair of students
- counters, 18 in one color and 18 in another or 36 two-color counters, per pair of students
- pencils, 1 per pair of students
- *Connect Four* Game Board (REPRODUCIBLE 12), 1 per pair of students
- *Connect Four* Game Directions (REPRODUCIBLE G-9), 1 per pair of students

Related Games
Game 10: Coordinates Secrecy (A Graphing Game)

Game 13: Four Square (Plotting Points)

Key Questions
- What does the first number of the coordinates represent? Which way do you travel from the origin?
- What does the second number indicate and in what direction do you travel?
- Show me the *x*-axis. Show me the *y*-axis.

Teaching Directions

Part I: The Connection

Relate the game to students' ongoing work.

Locate a Connect Four game by Milton Bradley and bring it to class. Ask students, "How many of you have played Connect Four or are familiar with it?" Share that the game they will be learning to play is similar to Connect Four in that it is played on a grid and the goal is to achieve four in a row.

Part II: The Teaching

Introduce and model the game to students.

1. Gather students in two concentric circles (one seated and one standing) around a table or seat them on the floor. Display the *Connect Four* Game Board (REPRODUCIBLE 12). Review the *x*- and *y*-axes with students. Consider using a memory technique like, "The letter X crosses and the *x*-axis goes across. The capital letter Y is made with a line that goes vertically and the *y*-axis goes vertically."

2. Tell students that they will be rolling a die to determine an ordered pair of numbers called coordinates. Explain, "You will roll the die twice. The number of the first roll will determine how far to travel on the *x*-axis and the number of the second roll will determine how far to move on the *y*-axis."

3. Ask a student volunteer to roll the die. Record the number. Ask the volunteer to roll the die once more. Record the second number. Separate the two numbers with a comma and reinforce that these numbers are the coordinates.

4. Next, using the coordinate plane on the game board, model how to move across and then up the axes per the coordinates. Place a counter at the intersection of the coordinates.

5. Repeat Steps 3 and 4, this time placing a different-color counter on the game board to mark the coordinates. Following is an

LEARNING TARGETS

Post the game's Learning Targets for students to see. This helps reinforce what students are responsible for learning as they play the game.

Grade 5:

- I understand that an ordered pair of numbers is called coordinates.

- I know that the names of the two axes are *x* and *y*.

- I know that the first number in the coordinates indicates how far to travel from the origin on the *x*-axis.

- I know that the second number in the coordinates indicates how far to travel up or down the *y*-axis.

- I can graph points on a coordinate plane to solve real-world and mathematical problems.

TECHNOLOGY TIP
Using an Interactive Whiteboard

If available, use an interactive whiteboard to model this game. Access the mathematics tools and select a coordinate grid with just Quadrant I and place it on a page. Then get two different colors of small circles from the tools (a stamp tool works, too) and infinitely clone both. Lastly, get an interactive die. Place all three items near the bottom of the same page.

TEACHING TIPS

Recording Moves

When modeling how to play this game, make sure to record the coordinates where all students can see them. Double-check students' understanding: do they understand that the first number represents the *x*-coordinate and the second number, the *y*-coordinate?

Using the Dice for Modeling Purposes

For modeling purposes, use a demonstration-size dice or use the dice on an interactive whiteboard. This ensures that every student can see the number rolled.

TEACHING TIP

Making Math Memorable

Consider revisiting the words *vertical, horizontal,* and *diagonal.* To help students remember them, write each word to visually represent its meaning:

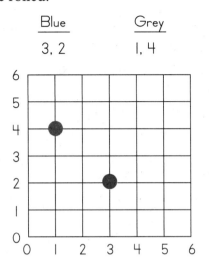

example of a game in which 3, 2 and 1, 4 were rolled:

```
      Blue        Grey
      3, 2        1, 4
```

6. Continue modeling the game with students. Get as many students involved as possible. One can roll the die twice, another can record the coordinates, and a third can move along both axes on the game board and place a counter at the intersection of the coordinates.

7. It is possible that a player may roll the same coordinates as those already marked on the game board by another player. If and when this happens, that player loses their turn.

8. Explain to students that the game is won by placing four counters in a row on the game board. The row may be vertical, horizontal, or diagonal.

9. Determine whether students understand the concept of the game by inserting a quick formative assessment such as thumbs-up. If no player has won yet, ask a comprehension question like, "Who can name what move on the coordinate grid would make a win for black or blue?"

```
horizontal    v    d
              e    i
              r      a
              t       g
              i        o
              c         n
              a          a
              l           l
```

Part III: Active Engagement
Engage students to ensure they understand how to play the game.

10. Now give students an opportunity to play the game in pairs. Each pair of students will need a *Connect Four* Game Board (REPRODUCIBLE 12), 36 colored counters (18 of each color) or 36 two-color counters, and a pencil for recording their coordinates. If a copy of *Connect Four* Game Directions (REPRODUCIBLE G-9) has not been distributed, this would also be the time to do so.

11. As students are playing, circulate. Note any misunderstandings that might be happening. Revisit, as needed, the procedural portions of the game, like the *x*-axis going across and the *y*-axis going up, the *x* being the first number in the coordinate pair and the *y* being the second.

12. Allow students to play for a specified amount of time. This means that some may finish a game and begin another while others may not complete a game.

Part IV: The Link
Students play the game independently.

13. Set students up for independent practice with the game. Designate and share a storage space for all the *Connect Four* materials. This encourages students to be self-sufficient in gathering the materials whenever there is time allotted to independently play the game.

TEACHING TIP
Formative Assessment
Formative assessments are necessary to gauge student understanding. They may be used before, during, or after a lesson. In the case of demonstrating this game, a formative assessment is recommended to determine if students are ready to play independently. Consider a quick thumbs-up assessment. Ask students, "Do you feel you understand the game enough to play on your own?" Have students put their thumbs up to indicate, "Yes, I completely understand. I know this," and thumbs down if "No, I need more time. I don't understand all the steps yet." Students may also show a thumbs-out to indicate uncertainty, "I mostly understand; however, I need to see a bit more demonstration." If the majority of students do not respond with a thumbs-up, continue guided teaching of the game.

TEACHING TIP
Pairing Students
The game of *Connect Four* involves both skill and luck; therefore, randomly pairing students will suffice. You might have students select their partners or use a classroom management routine such as pulling sticks labeled with students' names.

DIFFERENTIATING YOUR INSTRUCTION
No Dice
For students needing more challenge, have them play a "no dice" version of the game. In this version, students rely on logic rather than luck as they select coordinates, record them, and play to win or play to block the other from connecting four in a row.

MATH WORKSHOP AND SUMMARIZING THE EXPERIENCE

After students have had several days to practice the game of *Connect Four*, introduce more vocabulary terms like coordinate plane and origin and revisit *x*- and *y*-axis. A fun and memorable way of doing this is by using song. Just as the alphabet was learned and memorized through song, learning terms to a tune help tap into the episodic memory pathway aiding in making learning stick. One site that has a song that does this is numberock. com. There is a free version. Click on the Data and Graphs tab and select the Coordinate Plane Quadrant 1 video/song. Be prepared for your students to request to watch the video more than once. Encourage them to sing along— even move—to the music.

ASSESSMENT

After students have had multiple opportunities to practice the game independently, consider using the *Connect Four* Assessment (**REPRODUCIBLE 13**) to further check for their understanding of graphing points on a coordinate plane. Students should be able to explain that the first number indicates how far to travel from the origin in the direction of one axis and the second number indicates how far to travel in the direction of the second axis.

Coordinates Secrecy
(A Graphing Game)

Overview

In this game students practice graphing points on a coordinate plane in an attempt to pinpoint secret coordinates. Players make guesses and place their guesses on the coordinate plane; the player who knows the secret coordinates records the guesses and provides information ("clues") as to whether any part of the guesses is in common with the secret coordinates. The objective of the game is to share and gain enough information to identify the secret coordinates.

Materials

- *Coordinates Secrecy* Recording Chart and Game Board 1 (REPRODUCIBLE 14), 1 per group of 2–4 students

- pencils, 1 per group of 2–4 students

- *Coordinates Secrecy* Game Directions (REPRODUCIBLE G-10), 1 per group of 2–4 students

Related Games

Game 9: Connect Four (A Graphing Game)

Game 11: Coordinate Tic-Tac-Toe

Recommended Grade 5

Time Instruction: 30–45 minutes
Independent Play: 10–20 minutes

TEACHING TIP
Maximizing Game Board Use
To conserve paper, copy the *Coordinates Secrecy* Recording Chart and Game Board 1 (REPRODUCIBLE 14) onto both sides of a sheet, so students can use it for two games. Or laminate it and have students use dry erase markers instead of pencils when playing the game, so the recording sheet and game board can be wiped clean each time and reused (you only want to do this if you don't expect students to submit the work they've done).

LEARNING TARGETS

Post the game's Learning Targets for students to see. This helps reinforce what students are responsible for learning as they play the game.

Grade 5:

- I understand that an ordered pair of numbers is called coordinates.
- I know that the names of the two axes are x and y.
- I know the first number in the coordinates indicates how far to travel from the origin on the x-axis.
- I know the second number in the coordinates indicates how far to travel up or down the y-axis.
- I can graph points on a coordinate plane to solve real-world and mathematical problems.

TEACHING TIPS

Displaying the Recording Chart and Game Board

There are several ways to display the recording chart and game board during the modeling part of this lesson. You could re-create both using graph chart paper. Or you can project the images onto a screen. If you are using an interactive whiteboard, scan the recording chart and game board, project the images onto the whiteboard, and turn on the ink layer so you can interact with them.

The Secret Coordinates

Write the secret coordinates on a piece of paper that students cannot see through; construction paper works well as it is a heavier weight and difficult to see through even when using a marker.

Key Questions

- What do you know about the coordinates so far?
- If there is a "1" recorded in the digit column of the recording chart, what does this mean?
- Which axis does the first number in the coordinates correspond to? Which axis does the second number in the coordinates correspond to?
- Select one of the plotted points on the coordinate plane. Which coordinates on the chart describe this point?

Teaching Directions

Part I: The Connection

Relate the game to students' ongoing work.

Share a map with students. The map should be something familiar to students such as a map of their local mall, bike trails, or subway routes. The map could also be a map of the state you live in or of your school (many classrooms have a map of the school posted near the door with the emergency plan noted). Ask, "How many of you have seen the words 'You are here' on a map?" If students have never taken note of this, show them such on a map. Explain that one way the "you are here" point might be plotted is through coordinates. Continue, "Today we will be playing a game using coordinates. For those of you who have played Battleship either online or the board game with the ships and pegs, the game *Coordinates Secrecy* is played in a similar manner."

Part II: The Teaching

Introduce and model the game to students.

1. Begin by displaying an enlarged version of the *Coordinates Secrecy* Recording Chart and Game Board 1 (REPRODUCIBLE 14). Make sure all students can clearly see it.

2. Point out that there are two different resources that will be used for this game; the first is a recording chart for tracking coordinate guesses; the second is the game board—a coordinate plane to plot the coordinate guesses.

3. The best way to demonstrate this game is through example. Tell students you have a secret set of coordinates in mind that they will need to guess. Without showing the students your coordinates, write the coordinates on a piece of paper, with the word *secret* above them in large enough print so that later, when you reveal the coordinates, the entire class will be able to see them.

4. Place your "secret coordinates" paper face-down on a table or desk or affix it to the wall or board with the backside facing students.

5. Emphasize to students their task is to figure out the secret coordinates. To do this, they will need to guess coordinates and plot their guesses on the game board. Share with students that, "After each guess, I will tell you if either number is correct and if either number is in the right order." Further explain that in this game, there are no doubles allowed so co-ordinates like 1, 1 or 5, 5 or 7, 7 cannot be the secret coordinates nor can be used as guesses.

6. Invite students to guess the secret coordinates. Have a student plot the guess on the game board (coordinate plane), then read the plane and record the coordinates in the Coordinates column of the recording sheet. Ask students, "Did you read the coordinates on the plane correctly?" If so, fill out the Number and Order columns of the recording chart as appropriate. For example, if the secret coordinates are 3, 6 and students guess 4, 3, read the game board (coordinate plane) and record and explain to students: "One of the numbers in the coordinates is correct, so

TEACHING TIP
The Importance of Practice
Refrain from discussing strategies while students are initially learning to play the game. Students will come to a better sense of strategy through practice. Later in the week, after students have had many experiences in playing *Coordinates Secrecy*, give them the opportunity to reflect upon and share their thinking around strategies.

I am writing 1 in the number column of the recording sheet. However, there are no coordinates in the right order, so I am writing 0 in the Order column:

Coordinates	Number	Order
4, 3	1	0

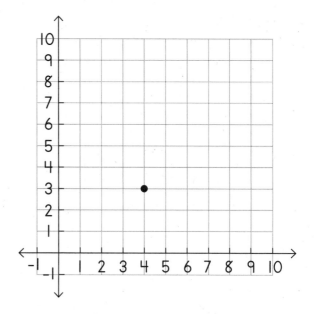

Respecting Everyone's Thinking

Whenever students are engaged in a collective classroom game, they are taking both a social and emotional risk in front of their peers. Establishing and nurturing a classroom environment in which students are respectful of their peers' thinking is paramount to maximizing participation and increasing engagement in the lesson. It may be necessary to remind students that when playing a game collectively, others will not always think the same way they do. They need to demonstrate kindness and control when someone offers a guess that they might not be thinking of or feel is a "wasted" guess.

7. Repeat Step 6, continuing to invite students to guess and plot the coordinates. After each guess, read what was plotted on the game board (coordinate plane), record the coordinates, and reveal "clues." Continuing with our example, this is what the recording chart might look like after a few more guesses:

Coordinates	Number	Order
4, 3	1	0
4, 5	0	0
3, 8	1	1
3, 7	1	1
3, 6	2	2

Note that in the chart, on the second coordinates guess, students were trying to determine which number was in the correct order. By keeping the 4 in the same order and replacing the 3 with a 5 they learned the 3 was in the correct place as the *x* in the coordinates. This is a very sophisticated strategy and unlikely unless students have had quite a bit of practice with this game or similar versions.

8. When teaching this game, to conserve time, you might not want to play until students guess the secrete coordinates. If this is the case, after a predetermined number of coordinate guesses, reveal the secret coordinates by turning over the paper that you wrote them on. Then refer to the recording chart and talk through each of the guesses. In the example given, the secret coordinates are 3, 6. So you might say, "In the first guess, 4, 3 one number is correct, the three; however, it is not in the right order. So, I recorded this information on the chart by placing a one in the Number column to show one number is correct, and I wrote a zero in the Order column to communicate that the digit is not in the correct order."

9. Move to explaining the second guess. Deemphasize the strategy, but instead focus on the recording. Say, "Next the coordinates 4, 5 were guessed. Neither of these digits are correct so I wrote a zero in the Number column as well as in the Order column."

10. Ask for volunteers to explain the other guesses listed on the chart, so students can gain practice in the reasoning of the recording.

Part III: Active Engagement

Engage students to ensure they understand how to play the game.

11. Now give students the opportunity to play the game in groups of three. Each group will need a copy of the *Coordinates Secrecy* Recording

TEACHING TIP
Grouping Students
Groups of two and four are OK too, but groups of three seem to work well for the lesson portion. Students can be randomly grouped for this game. If you have 30 students in your class, for example, numbering off 1–10 will provide you with 10 random groups of three if all the ones, all the twos, all the threes, and so forth become a group. The drawback of random grouping, however, is that students who don't work well together might end up in a group together. You know your students best; if needed, assign groups of three in advance.

TEACHING TIP
Remembering the Secret Coordinates

Students should each have an opportunity to be the player who holds the secret coordinates as well as be one of the players who guesses. Remind students that when it is their turn to think of secret coordinates, they need to write them down. Often students will use the back of the *Coordinates Secrecy* Recording Chart and Game Board 1 (**REPRODUCIBLE 14**) to jot down the secret coordinates.

TIME SAVER
Six Guesses Limit

Many teachers are under time constraints for subject matter lessons. If this is true of you, rather than having each of the three students in the group complete each game, consider having a limited amount of guesses for the secret coordinate before revealing it. Six guesses per game works well for students to get a feel for the game and allows for all students to practice both guessing and being the secret keeper and learning how to record in information on the *Coordinates Secrecy* Recording Chart.

DIFFERENTIATING YOUR INSTRUCTION
Game Board 2: Four Quadrants

After students have had many experiences with the game *Coordinates Secrecy*, consider offering a more challenging version in which students use all four quadrants of the coordinate plane and a +/− column is added to the recording chart. Students record the coordinates, number, and order just as before only now there is an additional column to report + and − and if 0, 1, or 2 are correct. See *Coordinates Secrecy* Recording Chart and Game Board 2 (**REPRODUCIBLE 15**).

Chart and Game Board 1 (**REPRODUCIBLE 14**) and a pencil.

12. As students are playing, circulate. Observe, clarify, and question students about the procedures of the game. You might inquire, "Tell me what you know so far." Or "What does the one in the Number column mean about this coordinates guess?" Make sure the holder of the secret coordinates is reading the guesses when they are plotted on the game board (coordinate plane), not being told the guesses (so they get practice in reading the coordinate plane, too!). For those who seem to have a firm grasp of the procedural part of the game, ask content questions such as, "Which axis does the first number in the coordinate pair represent? Which axis does the second number in the coordinates correspond to?" Or have students tell you which coordinates on the recording chart describe which point on the game board (coordinate plane).

13. Students should play at least three rounds of the game so they all gain experience in being the guesser as well as the player who holds the secret coordinates and reports out "clues."

Part IV: The Link
Students play the game independently.

14. Set students up for independent practice with the game. Designate and share a storage space for the *Coordinates Secrecy* materials. This encourages students to be self-sufficient in gathering the materials whenever there is time allotted to independently play the game. Also, as appropriate, make clear how groups should be formed and how many rounds of the game students should play.

MATH WORKSHOP AND SUMMARIZING THE EXPERIENCE

Teach this game at the beginning of the week to the whole class, then make it an integral part of your math workshop (for more on math workshop, see *Math Workshop* by Jennifer Lempp). Once students have had ample time to play the game, bring them back together as a class and have students reflect on both the Learning Targets and strategies. This could be done using a math journal or exit card (notecard) in response to a question like: Explain your strategy when playing *Coordinates Secrecy*. In the coordinates 4, 5 which number represents the x-axis and which one represents the y-axis? Why do you think this?

Another way to reflect on this game as a class is to create a classroom vocabulary chart. Write the term, definition, and an illustration to represent it. Your chart may look something like this:

Term	Definition	Illustration
coordinate	The ordered pair that states the location on a coordinate place used to described location and/or position.	2, 1
x-axis	The horizontal axis in a coordinate plane.	
y-axis	The vertical axis in a coordinate plane.	

A CHILD'S MIND
Logical Reasoning and Strategies

When playing the differentiated version of *Coordinates Secrecy* students may rely on logical reasoning and guess the same coordinates four consecutive times with only changing the positive and negative. This eliminates three of the four quadrants from the beginning of the game and they can put their energy and efforts toward guessing coordinates in one quadrant rather than four. One fifth grader started every round by guessing 2, 4 then −2, 4 then −2, −4 then 2, −4 in order to to learn which quadrant the secret coordinates were in: quadrant I, II, III or IV.

Coordinate Tic-Tac-Toe

Recommended Grades 3–5

Time Instruction: 45–60 minutes
Independent Play: 20–30 minutes

 TIME SAVER
Reusable Game Boards
Instead of making consumable copies of the *Coordinate Tic-Tac-Toe* Game Board, laminate a set or place copies in plastic sleeves and provide dry erase markers to use during game play.

Overview

This game is played much like the classic tic-tac-toe. However, in this version, students mark their moves (Xs and Os) on a coordinate plane instead of a regular tic-tac-toe board. Students gain early practice in graphing by taking turns choosing and plotting points and then recording the coordinates of their move using the correct notation. The first player to get four in a row—horizontally, vertically, or diagonally—is the winner.

Materials

- pencil, 1 per student
- *Coordinate Tic-Tac-Toe* Recording Chart and Game Board 1 (REPRODUCIBLE 16), 1 per student
- *Coordinate Tic-Tac-Toe* Game Directions (REPRODUCIBLE G-11), 1 per pair of students

Related Games

Game 9: Connect Four (A Graphing Game)

Game 10: Coordinates Secrecy
(A Graphing Game)

Game 17: Line Plot Tic-Tac-Toe

Key Questions

- Where is the origin and how is it named?
- Which axis is *x* and which is *y*?
- Which number in a coordinate pair represents *x*?
- Which number in a coordinate pair represents *y*?

- Where is this point on the coordinate plane? [Gesture to a pair of coordinates on the T-chart found on *Coordinate Tic-Tac-Toe* Recording Chart and Game Board 1 (REPRODUCIBLE 16)].

- Which coordinates on the T-chart represent this point [point to an X or O on the coordinate plane]?

Teaching Directions
Part I: The Connection
Relate the game to students' ongoing work.

Draw a classic tic-tac-toe game board large enough for all students to see:

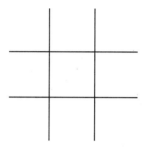

Ask students, "What game might you be familiar with that uses a board like this?" Once students answer, "Tic-tac-toe!" ask, "Who has played tic-tac-toe before?" Find out what students know about playing the game. Then discuss how, in the traditional game, Xs and Os are used to mark moves on the board. Tell students that in today's game, *Coordinate Tic-Tac-Toe*, the game board will be a coordinate plane and though Xs and Os will still be used to mark moves, these markers will be placed on the intersecting points that are created with the parallel and perpendicular lines on a coordinate plane.

Part II: The Teaching
Introduce and model the game to students.

1. Tell students that they will be playing the game *Coordinate Tic-Tac-Toe* with a partner. Distribute the *Coordinate Tic-Tac-Toe* Recording Chart and Game Board 1

LEARNING TARGETS
Post the game's Learning Targets for students to see. This helps reinforce what students are responsible for learning as they play the game.

Grade 3:
- I understand an ordered pair of numbers is called coordinates.

Grade 4:
- I know that the names of the two axes are *x* and *y*.
- I know that the first number in the coordinates indicates how far to travel from the origin on the *x*-axis.
- I know that the second number in the coordinates indicates how far to travel up or down the *y*-axis.

Grade 5:
- I can graph points on a coordinate plane to solve real-world and mathematical problems.

TECHNOLOGY TIP
Using an Interactive Whiteboard

If you are using an interactive whiteboard in your classroom, select a Quadrant I coordinate plane grid from the math toolkit. Create a page with the coordinate grid and a T-chart that matches the game board.

TEACHING TIP
Displaying the Game Board

One way to display the game board is outlined in the Technology Tip above. Alternatively, you may choose to project the game board on another device. If you wish to create your own game board, a piece of chart graph paper works well (simply highlight the x- and y-axes and label 1–10 on both axes). Include a T-chart to the left of the enlarged coordinate plane, so that the chart graph paper looks exactly like the game board the students have. Label one column X and one column O.

TEACHING TIP
Making Math Memorable

Having students engage several senses at once helps with memory retention. When asked to trace each axis while stating the name of the axis, students see, hear, and feel. The more senses that students engage while learning, the more they may learn.

(REPRODUCIBLE 16), one copy per student. Also clearly display an enlarged version for everyone to see.

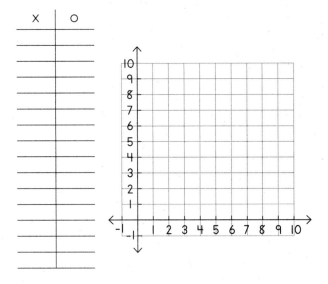

2. Focus students' attention on the coordinate plane, and ask, "What do you notice about the game board?" Responses might be:

   - "It has numbers one to ten going vertically and horizontally."

   - "It is Quadrant One of a coordinate plane."

   - "The grid is formed with parallel and perpendicular lines."

3. Highlight students' observations on the enlarged game board.

4. Review the terms x-axis and y-axis to further familiarize students with the game board. Have students find the x-axis and trace it with their finger. Do the same for the y-axis. Observe students doing this on their individual copies of the game board; do they all understand that the x-axis runs horizontally, and the y-axis runs vertically?

5. Instruct students to find the origin of the coordinate plane. If students are unfamiliar with the term or have not yet been introduced to the word *origin*, share with them that "The origin is the point where the x- and y-axes

intersect. We use this point as the starting place when finding points on the coordinate plane."

6. Next, direct students' attention to the T-chart on the game board. Emphasize that this is an important part of the game board; it is where each move is recorded. Explain, "Each time a player determines where to move, they must correctly record their coordinates and state the coordinates out loud to the other players."

7. Once students are familiar with the game board, start playing. First designate yourself as Player 1 and the students as Player 2. Explain, "Player 1's moves will be recorded with an X and Player 2's with an O.

8. Next walk students through your turn as Player 1. As you place your X on the coordinate plane, state, "I am picking a point on the coordinate plane and marking it with my mark, an X." Then say, "Now I have to figure out the correct coordinates for the point I marked and record them in the T-chart under column X. Hmmm . . . my coordinate points are three, four." Emphasize that players should always read their coordinates out loud when recording to keep all other players engaged and learning as well.

9. Now introduce how one wins the game. "Just like in tic-tac-toe, the goal is to get Xs or Os in a row either vertically, horizontally, or diagonally; however, in the traditional game of tic-tac-toe the goal is to attain three in a row; in this game, the winner must have four in a row. The reasoning for this is usually revealed when playing a round so let's continue."

10. Play three rounds, or six moves total using the enlarged version of the game board. Each time it is Player 2's turn, have a student volunteer to place an O on the coordinate plane, then work with her classmates to determine and record the coordinates. After three

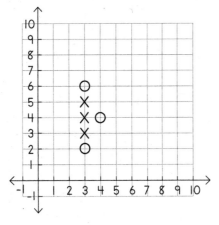

X	O
3, 4	4, 4
3, 3	3, 2
3, 5	3, 6

TEACHING TIPS
Emphasize Collaboration

For Part III, "Active Engagement," students should test the game out with their partner, not playing against him or her. The goal is for students to work together in understanding how to play the game and the math that is involved. When students have the opportunity to play the game independently (Part IV), they can play each other.

The Importance of Asking Questions

Asking key questions assists you in understanding how or if students are developing strategies. When you ask key questions, students get to hear other students' thinking and further develop their own understanding of the content.

DIFFERENTIATING YOUR INSTRUCTION
Groups of Four

If some students are not yet ready to play this game in pairs, team up two pairs to create a group of four to play.

rounds, students might see why three in a row will not work well as the winning combo, as it is too easy for the first player, the X, to win (this is because there are more options on the *Coordinate Tic-Tac-Toe* Recording Chart and Game Board than the traditional one). See the example (next to this step) of the first six moves from a demonstration round, teacher (Player 1 or X) versus the class (Player 2 or O) collectively.

11. Continue playing teacher versus the class until a player makes the winning move. Use this instructional time to talk through common mistakes (note that students sometimes mix up the x and the y in a pair of coordinates). Tell students that both players need to concur that the ordered pair (coordinates) match the location on the coordinate plane. You might say to students, "Make sure both players agree that the x, y on the T-chart match the location of the X or O on the coordinate plane, which is your game board (REPRODUCIBLE 16). If you don't agree, that player, has one chance to correct the mistake and then loses their turn."

Part III: Active Engagement
Engage students to ensure they understand how to play the game.

12. Now give students the opportunity to explore the game in pairs using the game boards they were given at the beginning of the lesson.

13. Set a clock or timer for a predetermined amount of time (recommend 10–15 minutes) for students to play. Should they complete a game, make sure they have another copy of the game board available.

14. As students are playing, circulate. Clarify misunderstandings and confirm correct play. Ask questions to check students' understanding (see "Key Questions," page 58).

Part IV: The Link

Students play the game independently.

15. Set students up for independent practice with the game. If students don't already have the directions, distribute the *Coordinate Tic-Tac-Toe* Game Directions (REPRODUCIBLE G-11). Highlight the Variations part of the directions as some students will be ready for these variations right away.

16. Designate and share a storage area for the copies of the *Coordinate Tic-Tac-Toe* Recording Chart and Game Board 1 (REPRODUCIBLE 16). This encourages students to be self-sufficient in gathering the materials whenever there is time allotted to independently play the game.

> ## MATH WORKSHOP AND SUMMARIZING THE EXPERIENCE
> Teach this game at the beginning of the week to the whole class, then make it an integral part of your math workshop (for more on math workshop, see *Math Workshop* by Jennifer Lempp). Come together later in the week and hold a discussion. Pose the question, "What sorts of strategy did you employ in the game of *Coordinate Tic-Tac-Toe*?" or "Was skill, luck, or strategy involved in the game? Explain."

TEACHING TIPS
The Importance of Practice
After several rounds of play, students might also get a sense of how much of the game depends on skill or strategy. Refrain from discussing these topics during the teaching part of the lesson. The purpose is to give students as much practice as possible first; they will then have the opportunity to come back later and discuss their experiences after they have played the game independently over a period of time.

Pairing Students
When pairing students for this game, place students of similar ability together. When students of similar ability work together, the speed of the game will be both comfortable and engaging for the students.

TEACHING TIP
Play It at Home!
The game *Coordinate Tic-Tac-Toe* can be played easily at home. For home use, *Coordinate Tic-Tac-Toe* needs only a copy of the game board and a pencil. Send home copies of the *Coordinate Tic-Tac-Toe* Game Directions (REPRODUCIBLE G-11) as necessary.

Desktop Shuffleboard
(A Measurement Game)

Recommended Grades 2–5

Time   Instruction: 45–60 minutes
Independent Play: 20–30 minutes

LEARNING TARGETS

Post the game's Learning Targets for students to see. This helps reinforce what students are responsible for learning as they play the game.

Grade 2:
· I can measure to the nearest inch or centimeter.

Grade 3:
· I can measure lengths to the nearest half and fourth of an inch.

· I can generate measurement data and place it in a line plot.

Grades 4 and 5:
· I can measure lengths to the nearest half, fourth, and eighth of an inch.

· I can generate measurement data and place it in a line plot.

Overview

In this game students take turns sliding a playing card across a flat surface, like a desk or table, with the goal of getting the card as close to the opposite edge as possible, without the card falling off. Students then measure and record the distance from where the card stopped to the edge of the table. After each student has had ten turns, students add up their measurements; the student with the lowest sum is the winner. As a final activity, there is the option for students to use their measurements to create a line plot.

Materials

- playing cards, 1 card per pair of students

- rulers, 1 per student

- pencils, 1 per student

- notebook paper

- *Desktop Shuffleboard* Recording Sheet 1 (REPRODUCIBLE 18), 1 per student

- dry erase markers

- orange pattern blocks

- new unsharpened pencils

- *Desktop Shuffleboard* Recording Sheet 2 (REPRODUCIBLE 19), 1 per pair of students

- *Desktop Shuffleboard* Game Directions (REPRODUCIBLE G-12), 1 per pair of students

Related Games

Game 8: Compare (Measurement Version)
Game 15: Go the Distance
(Customary and Metric Versions)

Key Questions

- What is the measurement to the nearest inch (or centimeter)? Show me how you know this.

- What is the measurement to the nearest $\frac{1}{2}$ or $\frac{1}{4}$ inch? Show me how you determined this.

- What is the measurement to the nearest $\frac{1}{8}, \frac{1}{4}$, and $\frac{1}{2}$ of an inch? Show me how you know this.

- Show me where you start to measure when you use a measuring tool like a ruler. (Note: Students often measure from the end of the ruler rather than where the zero hash mark is.)

Teaching Directions

Part I: The Connection

Relate the game to students' ongoing work.

Ask students, "Who has ever played Ping-Pong, pool, or shuffleboard?" Find out what students know about playing these games. What do the games have in common? Students may point out that each game involves moving an object (balls or discs) and a flat surface. Focus in on the game of shuffleboard. Perhaps play a brief online video of a shuffleboard game in action. Point out the use of a weighted disc. If available, consider bringing a disc to class to share with students. Finally, let students know that today they will be engaged in a math game called *Desktop Shuffleboard*. Explain that in this version of shuffleboard students will be using a playing card rather than weighted discs. Classroom tables (or desks) will serve as the board and students will need to use their measuring skills.

Part II: The Teaching

Introduce and model the game to students.

1. Give each student a ruler and begin a review of measurement appropriate to grade level: if teaching grade 2, review inch and centimeter; if teaching grade 3, review where the

TEACHING TIP
Student Engagement
Consider using the strategy turn and talk. Students turn and talk with their neighbor about what they know about shuffleboard. Put a time constraint on this sharing strategy; make it quick while meeting the social needs of students.

TIME SAVER
Materials for Use with Reproducible 18

When introducing the game to students using **REPRODUCIBLE 18**, you will need to have some classroom items available. Those items are: dry erase markers, orange pattern blocks, new (unsharpened) pencils, notebook or copy paper. No need to have an abundance of each as students will be moving about the room measuring the items and can complete the tasks in any order.

TEACHING TIP
Formative Assessment

A formative assessment is used to inform instruction. Doing a quick formative assessment at this part of the lesson helps you get insight into whether students have the necessary knowledge to play the game. Are students appropriately using their rulers and measuring accurately? Students might work in pairs for this assessment.

TECHNOLOGY TIP
Using an Interactive Whiteboard

When reviewing students' measurement findings as a class, consider using an interactive whiteboard to create a T-chart matching the chart on **REPRODUCIBLE 18**.

TEACHING TIP
Displaying the Recording Sheet

One way to display the recording sheet is outlined in the Technology Tip above. Alternatively, you may choose to project the recording sheet on another device. You may also create your own enlarged version of the sheet by drawing the T-chart on the board.

marks for $\frac{1}{2}$ and $\frac{1}{4}$ inch are on the ruler; if teaching grades 4 or 5, also include a review of the $\frac{1}{8}$-inch mark.

2. Once students have reviewed the appropriate markings on their rulers, conduct a quick formative assessment. Do this by distributing a copy of the *Desktop Shuffleboard (A Measurement Game)* Recording Sheet 1 (**REPRODUCIBLE 18**) to each student. Using an enlarged version of the recording sheet, go through the directions with students; students should walk around the classroom, find each item on the list (dry erase marker, orange pattern block, new [unsharpened] pencil, and paper) measure it, and record their measurements. Explain that they will need to measure each item in both inches and centimeters.

3. After students have moved around the room and collected their measurements, bring them back together, record their findings on your enlarged copy of the recording sheet, and discuss as needed. Your results might look something like this:

ITEM	MEASUREMENT
Dry Erase Marker	inches: $5\frac{1}{2}$ centimeters: 14
Orange Pattern Block	inch: 1 centimeters: 2.5
New (Unsharpened) Pencil	inches: $7\frac{1}{2}$ centimeters: 19
Width of Paper	inches: $8\frac{1}{2}$ centimeters: 21.5
Length of Paper	inches: 11 centimeters: 28

4. Once students have successfully practiced measuring, gather them around a desk or table to model the game.

5. Point out that for this game two sides of the table need to be clearly designated—the start side and the finish side. To start, place a playing card on the start side of the table, with the top edge aligned to the start edge:

6. Explain to students that they will take turns sliding the playing card across a table. The goal is to get the card as close to the opposite edge (finish side) of the table as possible without it falling off. Demonstrate this, firmly yet gently pushing the card so it slides forward across the surface, as if it were a disc in a game of shuffleboard, aiming it toward the opposite end of the table.

7. Now share with students, "Where the card stops is where you will take a measurement." Move to the finish side of the table. Say, "Your measurement starting point is the tip or edge of the card that is closest to the finish side of the table. If the card slid sideways, this may be a corner. If it slid straight forward it will be the short side of the card." Continue, "Your measurement ending point is the finish side (edge) of the table." Depending on the grade level and Learning Target students are working toward, tell students the unit of measure and how accurate they must be (nearest inch, half inch, fourth of an inch, or

> **TEACHING TIP**
> ### Arranging Students
> For the modeling part of this game, have students make two concentric circles. In the first circle, students kneel or sit; in the second, students stand. This helps ensure everyone can view the demonstration area.

eighth of an inch). Demonstrate measuring the appropriate distance (see blue line in illustration below).

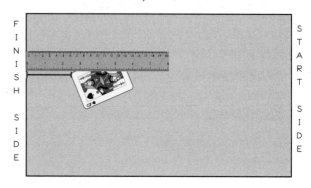

8. Now emphasize the importance of students recording their measurements. Say, "You will keep track of your measurements on a recording sheet." Show an enlarged version of the *Desktop Shuffleboard (A Measurement Game)* Recording Sheet 2 (REPRODUCIBLE 19). Write your name and the measurement from Step 7 in the first column of the sheet.

9. Now invite a student volunteer to take a turn sliding the card across the table, measuring, and recording the measurement in column 2, labeling it *The Class*. While the student is measuring the distance, ask the rest of the class to estimate what they think the distance is based on their prior knowledge.

10. Play more of the game, asking for a new student volunteer each time (and tasking the rest of the class with estimating the measurement) until there are several measurements recorded. Tell students that when playing the game, a game ends when each player has had ten turns. When modeling the game, students typically get a feel for the game after several turns.

11. Now explain how the game is scored. "Each player adds up the measurements in their column; the player with the lowest sum is the winner." Students may want to record their measurements using decimals to make for easy computation at the end of the game.

TEACHING TIP
Variation: Traditional Shuffleboard

In the original game of shuffleboard, part of the goal is to knock your opponent off the board. The goal of *Desktop Shuffleboard*, on the other hand, is for students to practice making measurements. However, as a variation, the game could be played to include the act of knocking opponents' cards off the table. In this case, each pair of students will need two cards. The card from the last play remains on the table each time, just through the next player's turn. If the card is knocked off by the slide of the next card, the player who knocked the card off can decide if their opponent adds 25 centimeters or 10 inches to their measurement sum or their opponent records a zero and they subtract 25 centimeters or 10 inches from their own running total. This allows for logical reasoning to weave into this version of the game. A note of caution: This variation will most likely result in students being louder as there is an additional element of competitiveness.

12. If a student slides the card such that it falls off the table, explain there is a penalty. "If your card falls off of the table, you have to add extra numbers to your total score. If you are measuring in centimeters, add twenty-five to your final sum. If you are measuring in inches, add ten to your final sum. Do this each time the card slides off the table."

Part III: Active Engagement
Engage students to ensure they understand how to play the game.

13. Now give students the opportunity to explore the game in pairs. Each pair should determine a playing space (desk or table), and have a playing card, ruler, pencil, and a copy of *Desktop Shuffleboard (A Measurement Game)* Recording Sheet 2 (REPRODUCIBLE 19).

14. As students are playing, circulate. Clarify misunderstandings and confirm correct play. Ask questions to check students' understanding (see "Key Questions," page 65). Remind students that a game is ten turns for each player. Once students have completed ten turns, remind them to add up their measurements—the player with the lowest sum is the winner.

Part IV: The Link
Students play the game independently.

15. Set students up for independent practice with the game. If students don't already have the directions, distribute the *Desktop Shuffleboard (A Measurement Game)* Game Directions (REPRODUCIBLE G-12).

16. Designate and share a storage area for the *Desktop Shuffleboard* materials. This encourages students to be self-sufficient in gathering the materials whenever there is time allotted to independently play the game.

TEACHING TIPS
Determining Playing Space
As students break up into pairs and decide on their playing space, encourage them to consider the location of other students. It would be best for students to be spread out, so that cards do not slide into and disrupt other students' games.

Create Your Own Recording Sheets
Students may create their own recording sheets by folding a single piece of notebook paper in half to form two columns, then labeling each column with their names.

Calculators or Pencil-and-Paper Computation?
Students may want to use a calculator for the final step of this game—adding up the ten measurements. Should they do so, strongly encourage estimation skills so that students question what the calculator displays. Often students will miss entering a decimal point, resulting in an answer that is escalated and incorrect.

MATH WORKSHOP AND
SUMMARIZING THE EXPERIENCE

Teach this game at the beginning of the week to the whole class, then make it an integral part of your math workshop (for more on math workshop, see *Math Workshop* by Jennifer Lempp). Collect students' recording sheets each time they play. Come together later in the week to reflect on the game and do a wrap-up activity. Task students with using the measurements they generated from the game to create a line plot. Give students their completed recording sheets and provide graph paper for creating the line plots (to maximize the use of graph paper, consider cutting the graph paper in half lengthwise, giving each pair of students a half, and instructing them to orient their papers the long way). If students are in third grade, it is recommended that this lead to another guided lesson, as it will be their first experience with displaying information using a line plot. Students in fifth grade should be able to achieve this Learning Target independently, however they will need to be aware of this expectation. As students are creating their line plots, circulate, asking questions to check their understanding, such as "What plot corresponds with this piece of measurement data?"

Four Square (Plotting Points)

Overview

This game was inspired by the classic playground game of Four Squares (played with four squares and a bouncy ball). In the math classroom adaptation of the game, instead of bouncing a ball, students plot coordinates. The four squares are four quadrants of a coordinate plane. To determine the coordinates to plot, a player rolls four dice: two with faces labeled + and – and the other two with faces labeled *1–6*. The player then creates and plots a playable coordinate combination from what is rolled. This is a four-player game and each player has a quadrant. Two main rules apply:

> Rule 1: The coordinate pair you choose to plot cannot be in your quadrant.

> Rule 2: The coordinate pair you choose to plot cannot have already been plotted.

Play continues until a player cannot plot a playable coordinate combination from his or her roll; when this is the case, all other players score a point, the game board is cleared, and a new round begins.

Materials

- dice (labeled +, +, +, –, –, –), 2 per group of 4 students
- dice (labeled *1–6*), 2 per group of 4 students
- small counters (dime-sized), 30–40 per group of 4 students
- pencils, 1 per group of 4 students
- paper, 1 per group of 4 students

Recommended Grade 5

Time Instruction: 45–60 minutes
Independent Play: 20–30 minutes

 TEACHING TIPS
Making +/– Dice
There are several options for making the +/– dice required in this game:

- Relabel existing dice: Use small round stickers to relabel existing dice.

- Label wooden cubes: Using stickers or a marker, label each face of a wooden cube.

- Use spinners: As an alternative to dice, create spinners. You can also use a combination of dice and spinners (for example, use two +/– dice and two spinners sectioned 1–6).

Quiet Dice
Rolling dice can create a lot of noise. To lessen the noise, use foam dice or pad students' workspaces with foam or fabric placemats.

Don't Have Counters?
Make Reusable Game Boards!
As an alternative to using counters, laminate the game board or place it in a plastic sleeve. Have students use dry erase markers to mark the game board. Yet another option, substitute counters for coins like pennies and nickels.

TIME SAVER
Managing Materials

Save time by organizing the dice and counters into sets prior to the lesson. Place each set in a quart-size sandwich bag. Bundle this with the *Four Square* Game Board **(REPRODUCIBLE 20)** and *Four Square* Game Directions **(REPRODUCIBLE G-13)**. Consider also making additional copies of the directions and posting them throughout the classroom for students to refer to during independent play.

LEARNING TARGETS

Post the game's Learning Targets for students to see. This helps reinforce what students are responsible for learning as they play the game.

Grade 5:

- I understand that an ordered pair of numbers is called coordinates.

- I know that the names of the two axes are x and y.

- I know that the first number in the coordinates indicates how far to travel from the origin on the x-axis.

- I know that the second number in the coordinates indicates how far to travel up or down the y-axis.

- I can graph points on a coordinate plane to solve real-world and mathematical problems.

Materials, continued

- *Four Square* Game Board (REPRODUCIBLE 20)
- *Four Square* Game Directions (REPRODUCIBLE G-13), 1 per group of 4 students

Related Games

Game 9: Connect Four (A Graphing Game)

Game 10: Coordinates Secrecy (A Graphing Game)

Game 11: Coordinate Tic-Tac-Toe

Key Questions

- What does the first number indicate in an ordered pair?

- What does the second number indicate in an ordered pair?

- How do you remember which axis is x and which one is y?

- What playable coordinates can you create from the dice you rolled?

- Why are you choosing to plot that coordinate pair?

- What are the coordinates of this point (gesture to a counter on the game board)?

Teaching Directions
Part I: The Connection

Relate the game to students' ongoing work.

Gather students on a playground or gymnasium floor to revisit the classic game *Four Square*. Make sure the ground or floor is marked accordingly (a standard Four Square area is one 10-foot-by-10-foot large square divided into four smaller squares; you can find online videos of people playing Four Square for further guidance). Ask students, "Who has played *Four Square*?" Find out what students know about playing the game. Have a student volunteer stand in each of the four squares (typically labeled *Jack, Queen, King,* and *Ace*) and model the game using a bouncy ball. Emphasize that you do not want the ball to bounce more than once in the square in which you are standing, nor do you want it to bounce on a line or go out of bounds.

Reveal to students, "The math game you will learn today is called *Four Square* and it is inspired by this game. Instead of a Four Square court, you will be playing on all four quadrants of a coordinate plane. You will use dice to determine your moves and counters to mark them."

Part II: The Teaching

Introduce and model the game to students.

1. Back in the classroom, gather students around a demonstration area—ideally a flat surface (desk, table, or floor).

2. Display the *Four Square* Game Board (REPRODUCIBLE 20) in the demonstration area. Introduce the names of the four quadrants and label them:

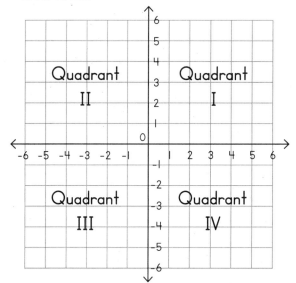

TEACHING TIPS
Arranging Students
For the modeling part of this game, have students make two concentric circles. In the first circle, students kneel or sit; in the second, students stand. This ensures that everyone can view the demonstration area.

Displaying the Game Board
It's critical that the game board is big enough for all students to see it during the modeling part of the lesson. If needed, make an enlarged copy of **REPRODUCIBLE 20** or create your own enlarged version of the game board using poster-size graph paper.

3. Designate Quadrant I as your playing space and stand/sit so that Quadrant I is in front of you. Assign Quadrants II–IV to three other players (student volunteers) and have the players arrange themselves in front of their quadrant. Emphasize the importance of taking the time to set up like this for each game.

4. Do further review of the coordinate plane (game board). Remind students of the *origin* ("The origin is the point where the *x*- and *y*-axes intersect. We use this point as the starting place when finding points on the coordinate plane"). Share that perpendicular lines are called axes and they help define the coordinate plane. Revisit what coordinates indicate: "The first number indicates how far to travel to the left or the right of the origin and the second number indicates how far to travel up or down the second axis."

5. Explain that to play this game, players plot coordinates on the game board. Share with students how coordinates will be determined: a player rolls four dice. Show students the dice (two of the dice are regular 1–6 dice and the other two have symbol labels +/–). Ask students to inspect all faces of the dice. What have they discovered?

6. After reporting their findings, especially the learning that the second pair of dice each contain three positive and three negative symbols, continue sharing how the dice will be used to determine the coordinates in this game. For example, write 2, 5, +, – where everyone can see. Ask students, "Pretend this is what I rolled. What coordinates can be created from these four pieces of information?" Task students with determining all of the coordinate combinations.

7. List the combinations as students offer them. In this example, the various coordinate combinations are:

$$+2, -5$$

$$-2, +5$$

$$+5, -2$$

$$-5, +2$$

TEACHING TIP

Using Think-Pair-Share

Use a strategy like think-pair-share to discover the coordinate combinations. First ask students to think independently about the question. Next instruct them to pair up with a classmate and discuss their thinking. Lastly, students should share out loud with the class.

8. Now explain that to make a move in this game, you must pick a pair of coordinates (created from your roll of the dice) that when plotted follows two rules:

> Rule 1: The coordinate pair you choose to plot cannot be in your quadrant.

> Rule 2: The coordinate pair you choose to plot cannot have already been plotted.

9. Emphasize that the first player to start is always the player in Quadrant I; in this case, that player is you. Using the example and rules in Steps 6–8, muse out loud over what coordinate pair to plot. In the case of your pretend roll, you could choose any of the coordinate combinations to plot (this will not always be the case, as rounds of play will reveal).

10. Plot your chosen coordinate pair by placing a counter on it.

11. The player whose turn is next is the one whose quadrant you just plotted a point in. Have that student roll the dice, create a coordinate pair that abides to the two rules in Step 8, and plot the coordinates on the game board. Continue play for several more rounds. As you model the game with the student volunteers, involve all students by asking them to think of the coordinate combination they would create and use based on each roll of the dice.

12. As you play, you will eventually encounter a situation in which a roll of the dice produces no coordinate combinations that can be played. When this happens, all the players *but* the player in play score a point. Model how best to keep track of points: write each player's name on a piece of paper and write a tally mark under those players who just scored a point.

13. When points are scored, the game is "reset"— all counters are removed from the game board and another round starts (once again,

TEACHING TIP
Tracking Points
Encourage students to keep track of points by writing tally marks (hash marks) instead of say, the number 1 to mean 1 point. This way students can add to their score with ease as the game continues.

TEACHING TIPS

Formative Assessment

Formative assessments are necessary to gauge student understanding. They may be used before, during, or after a lesson. In the case of demonstrating this game, a formative assessment is recommended to determine if students are ready to play independently. Consider a quick thumbs-up assessment. Ask students, "Do you feel you understand the game enough to play on your own?" Have students put their thumbs up to indicate, "Yes, I completely understand. I know this," and thumbs down if "No, I need more time. I don't understand all the steps yet." Students may also show a thumbs-out to indicate uncertainty, "I mostly understand, however I need to see a bit more demonstration." If the majority of students do not respond with a thumbs-up, continue guided teaching of the game.

Providing Choice in Student Grouping

Having students self-select and form their own group of four is not always in the best interest of all students; however, you can introduce choice when grouping students. To do so, first have students choose a partner and then, as the teacher, "pair up" the pairs to form groups of four. This way you can offer students choice while still managing the groups, making sure there is a balance of personalities and mathematical understanding in each.

Groups of Four

Having students work in groups of four supports everyone in their math understanding. Twice as many brains at work leads to more correctness in plotting points. However, this setup may increase classroom noise substantially, especially when students are trying to choose a coordinate pair. Remember, classroom volume about mathematics is okay. Encourage students to share their thinking!

the player in Quadrant I starts). While it is unlikely, this may happen before every player has had a chance to play.

14. Continue the demonstration until all students have a firm grasp of the procedures of the game. Determine whether students understand the concept of the game by inserting a quick formative assessment such as thumbs-up.

Part III: Active Engagement

Engage students to ensure they understand how to play the game.

15. Now give students the opportunity to explore the game in groups of four. Each group should determine a playing space (desk, table, or floor with substantial space such that they can each be near their assigned quadrant), and have the necessary counters, dice, a pencil and paper for tracking scores, and a copy of the *Four Square* Game Board (REPRODUCIBLE 20). Emphasize that each student needs to sit or stand next to a quadrant on the game board; the player next to Quadrant I starts the game.

16. As students are playing, circulate. Clarify misunderstandings and confirm correct play. Remind students to keep track of their scores. Ask questions to check students' understanding (see "Key Questions," page 72).

Part IV: The Link

Students play the game independently.

17. Set students up for independent practice with the game. If students don't already have the directions, distribute the *Four Square* Game Directions (REPRODUCIBLE G-13).

18. Designate and share a storage area for the *Four Square* materials. This encourages students to be self-sufficient in gathering the materials whenever there is time allotted to independently play the game.

MATH WORKSHOP AND SUMMARIZING THE EXPERIENCE

Teach this game at the beginning of the week to the whole class, then make it an integral part of your math workshop (for more on math workshop, see *Math Workshop* by Jennifer Lempp). To make the learning even more memorable, have students actually play in a Four Square area marked on the gymnasium floor or on a playground. Label the four quadrants I, II, III, IV. When players move the bouncy ball into another player's quadrant, they must say the name of the quadrant. If they name it incorrectly, they are out and the next player in line rotates in to play. The general rules of Four Square still apply, like the ball cannot land on any lines or go out of the court. See instructional videos on YouTube for a quick review on how to play this timeless game.

ASSESSMENT

After students have had multiple opportunities to practice the game independently, use the *Four Square* Assessment **(REPRODUCIBLE 21)** to further check for their understanding.

TEACHING TIP
Groups of Two or Four

Once students are ready to play this game independently, you can have them play in groups of four or two. As modeled, when four players are playing, the order of play is determined by where the last point was plotted. If just two players are playing, play simply alternates back and forth no matter what quadrant the last move was made within. Playing with four players works best for the learning of the game, as there are more minds engaged in the play, and students can help each other with misunderstandings.

Geometry Go Fish

Recommended Grades 2–3

Time Instruction: 30–45 minutes
    Independent Play: 15–20 minutes

TEACHING TIPS
A Deck of Cards
For the purpose of this game, a deck of cards is one copy of each page of **REPRODUCIBLE 22**, totaling 30 cards.

Reusable Cards
To ensure the longevity of cards, use thick paper stock and/or laminate them. Store each deck in a quart-size sandwich bag.

Color-Coding Decks
To keep decks of cards from getting mixed up with other sets, use a different color of paper for each deck.

Overview
This game is a version of the classic game Go Fish. In *Geometry Go Fish*, players put aside pairs of cards with matching shapes. Then players take turns asking each other for shapes they need to make matching pairs. Play continues until all the cards in the deck are used up (paired) or until one player goes out by having no remaining cards to play. This game encourages practice with two-dimensional shapes; the included variation extends it to common three-dimensional shapes.

Materials
- *Geometry Go Fish* Cards, 2-D Shapes (**REPRODUCIBLE 22**), 1 deck per pair of students
- *Geometry Go Fish* Game Directions (**REPRODUCIBLE G-14**), 1 per pair of students

Related Games
Game 8: Compare (Measurement Version)

Key Questions
- Where might you see this shape outside of math class?
- Does this shape have lines of symmetry? How many?
- What might a four-sided shape be called?
- What attributes do these shapes have in common?

Teaching Directions
Part I: The Connection
Relate the game to students' ongoing work.

Ask students, "Have you gone fishing before?" Relate their knowledge or experiences of going fishing to the game of *Geometry Go Fish*. Tell students the "fishing pond" in the game is all the cards. They will be fishing for matching shapes. If some students have played the classic game of *Go Fish* before, be sure to distinguish between the two. Find out what students know about playing the traditional game.

Part II: The Teaching
Introduce and model the game to students.

1. Pair students up and distribute a deck of *Geometry Go Fish* Cards (REPRODUCIBLE 22) to each pair of students.

2. Instruct students, in pairs, to sort their deck of cards into two piles: an "I'm familiar with these shapes" pile and an "I'm uncertain about these shapes" pile. Students should try to name the shapes on the cards as they are sorting.

3. Circulate, observing students. Change up pairs should partners be incompatible in having similar knowledge of shapes.

4. After students have sorted through the cards and refreshed their memories on shapes, review as a class the shapes that seem to be most common in the "I'm uncertain about these shapes" piles.

5. Once the shapes have been reviewed, gather students in a demonstration area. Have a student volunteer be your partner in modeling the game. First show students how to shuffle and deal the cards, five per player.

6. After five cards are dealt to both your partner and you, place the remaining cards facedown in the middle of the playing area and gently

LEARNING TARGETS
Post the game's Learning Targets for students to see. This helps reinforce what students are responsible for learning as they play the game.

Grade 2:
- I can recognize shapes having specified attributes, such as a given number of angles or a given number of equal faces.
- I can identify triangles, quadrilaterals, pentagons, hexagons, octagons, and cubes.

Grade 3:
- I can reason with shapes and their attributes.
- I understand that shapes have different categories based on number of sides and/or angles.

TEACHING TIP
Pairing Students
For Parts II and III of this lesson, predetermine student pairs based on their like knowledge of shapes. Note that the procedures of this game are relatively easy to grasp as many students will have experience playing the traditional game of *Go Fish*. If this is the case, use Part II to focus on reviewing and introducing the shapes more so than the procedures.

TECHNOLOGY TIP
Using an Interactive Whiteboard
To review the shapes, you may use a deck of cards or, alternatively, use an interactive whiteboard. For the latter, select the shapes from the geometry file in the math toolkit or use the whiteboard stamps to produce the shapes. Type each of the names of the shapes separately and have students drag the names and place them next to the shape for an interactive matching review.

TEACHING TIP
Shuffling Cards
Younger students are typically not able to shuffle the cards. If this is the case, demonstrate how to mix the cards with your hands, being careful to keep all the cards facing the same direction (either facedown or faceup).

spread them out so that no two cards are touching, and all remain facedown. Call this the "fishing pond."

7. Next say out loud, "At the beginning of each game, each player looks at his or her hand and places any matches aside. Then you replenish those cards in your hand by picking up cards from the middle—the fishing pond; the number of cards you pick up should equate to the number you matched and set aside." This means it is possible that a player could have two matches (four cards) set aside.

8. Are there still matches? If so, place those aside as well. After setting matches aside a second time, players now proceed to ask each other for cards to make matches. Model this by asking the student volunteer, for example, "Do you have an octagon?" If the student does, the student must hand you her octagon card; pair it with yours and set the match aside. Continue asking the student for matches until she no longer has a card you're requesting. When this is the case, the student replies, "Go Fish" and you must draw a card from the middle. Place aside a match if it makes one. Your turn is then over.

9. Finally, share with students the two ways to win:

   • If a player has paired all of their cards and has no cards left in their hand, they are the winner.

   • If all the cards are played and no more pairs can be made, players add up the matched cards that they have set aside; the winner is the player with the most matches.

Part III: Active Engagement
Engage students to ensure they understand how to play the game.

10. Now give the students an opportunity to explore the game in pairs. Each pair should

TEACHING TIP
Determining Playing Space
As students move into pairs and decide on their playing space, encourage them to consider the location of other students. It would be best for students to be spread out, so that decks of cards do not get mixed up.

determine a playing space (desk, table, or floor) and have a deck of *Geometry Go Fish* cards (REPRODUCIBLE 22).

11. As students are playing, circulate. Clarify misunderstandings and confirm correct play. Ask questions about pairs of cards that have already been matched to check students' understanding (see "Key Questions," page 78). Make notes on which students might be better paired with other students.

12. Set a certain amount of time like 10–15 minutes for the game to be practiced before proceeding to Part IV.

Part IV: The Link

Students play the game independently.

13. Set students up for independent practice with the game. If students don't already have the directions, distribute the *Geometry Go Fish* Game Directions (REPRODUCIBLE G-14).

14. Designate and share a storage area for the *Geometry Go Fish* cards. This encourages students to be self-sufficient in gathering the materials whenever there is time allotted to independently play the game.

MATH WORKSHOP AND SUMMARIZING THE EXPERIENCE

Teach this game at the beginning of the week to the whole class, then make it an integral part of your math workshop (for more on math workshop, see *Math Workshop* by Jennifer Lempp). Later in the week, use the cards once again, this time taping one to the back of each student's shirt (students should not see or be told the shape taped to their back). Instruct students to mingle about the classroom, asking others to describe the shape on their back to eventually find a match. When this happens, matched students sit down.

TEACHING TIP
The Importance of Asking Questions

Asking key questions assists you in understanding how or if students are developing strategies. Key questions also prompt students to hear each other's thinking and further develop their own understanding of the content.

DIFFERENTIATING YOUR INSTRUCTION
Describe the Shape's Attributes

For those students who need more of a challenge, change the game so students can only ask their partner for a shape by describing its attributes (they cannot use the actual name of the shape). This encourages the use of additional math vocabulary; students may use descriptions like parallel lines, perpendicular lines, or the presence or absence of angles of a specific size. They may also use lines of symmetry to help define a shape. For example, to describe a square, a student might say, "If you fold this shape from corner to opposite corner it will make a triangle." Or, when you fold it in half it becomes a rectangle, not a . . . ".

Go the Distance
(Customary and Metric Versions)

Recommended Grades 1–3

Time Instruction: 45–60 minutes
Independent Play: 20–30 minutes

Overview

There are two versions of this game, the customary version and the metric version. If playing the customary version, players take turns rolling two dice (labeled *1–6*) and deciding to record the sum of the rolled numbers in either inches or feet. After ten turns, the player closest to ten yards (thirty feet) without going over wins. If playing the metric version, players take turns rolling two dice (labeled *1–6*) and deciding whether to add or multiply the numbers generated. Next, they decide to record the sum or product in millimeters or centimeters. After ten turns, the player closest to one meter without going over wins. This lesson is written using the customary version. This game is adapted from the game *Roll for $1.00* and its variation, *Roll for 1*, both from *Math Games for Number and Operations and Algebraic Thinking*.

TEACHING TIPS

Don't Have Enough Dice?
If you do not have enough dice for two per pair of students, use spinners sectioned 1–6.

Quiet Dice
Rolling dice can create a lot of noise. To lessen the noise, use foam dice or pad students' workspaces with foam or fabric placemats.

Materials

- dice (labeled *1–6*), 2 per pair of students
- pencils, 2 per pair of students
- *Go the Distance* Recording Sheet (Customary Version) **(REPRODUCIBLE 24)**, 1 per student
- *Go the Distance* Game Directions **(REPRODUCIBLE G-15A)**, 1 per pair of students
- rulers, 2 per pair of students (optional)

Related Games

Game 8: Compare (Measurement Version)
Game 18: March to the Meter

Key Questions

- How are you deciding if a roll should be recorded as inches or feet?

- If you have 14* inches, what are the equivalent feet and inches? (*Substitute any number over 12 and less than 24.)

Teaching Directions
Part I: The Connection
Relate the game to students' ongoing work.

If this is students' first introduction to a measurement unit, introduce "body benchmarks." For example:

- an index finger from knuckle to knuckle is about an inch, and

- the distance from one's elbow to wrist (or fingertips) is about a foot.

With the understanding that body benchmarks range depending on the student, encourage students to find a body benchmark to connect with each unit of measure. This is both engaging and important for developing real-life estimation skills.

In addition to body benchmarks, offer different measurement tools for students to explore. These tools might include rulers, yard sticks, tape measures, and a measuring wheel (if you do not have a measuring wheel in your classroom, check with a physical education teacher).

Finally, take students outside to the football field or a parking lot (you can also remain inside and go to a place with a lot of space like a gymnasium). Have students, in teams, do ten-yard shuttle runs. Let students know that back in the classroom they will be playing a game using the same measurement.

Part II: The Teaching
Introduce and model the game to students.

1. Once back in the classroom, gather students around a table or demonstration area. Share

LEARNING TARGETS
Post the game's Learning Targets for students to see. This helps reinforce what students are responsible for learning as they play the game.

Grade 1:
- I can measure length as a whole number of length units.

Grade 2:
- I can measure and estimate lengths in standard units.

Grade 3:
- I can measure lengths using rulers marked with halves and fourths of an inch.

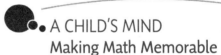

A CHILD'S MIND
Making Math Memorable
The episodic memory pathway is the "where you were when . . ." memory pathway in our brains. Creating a memorable moment in a place besides the classroom aids in students' learning retention. Another brain-compatible strategy in making learning "stick" is engaging students in movement while learning.

TEACHING TIPS

Arranging Students

For the modeling part of this game, have students make two concentric circles. In the first circle, students kneel or sit; in the second, students stand. This ensures that everyone can view the demonstration area.

The Metric Version

This lesson is written to introduce the customary version of the game; however, the lesson could be presented similarly for the metric version. To introduce the metric version, have students place a meter stick on the floor and, in small groups, practice doing standing long jumps next to it. Then, when playing the game, students roll the dice and have the choice of adding or multiplying the numbers and recording the sum or product in millimeters or centimeters. The goal of the game is to be closest to one meter without going over. Students are asked to share either the sum or the product of the two numbers and the goal of the game is to be closest to one meter without going over. For the metric version, use **REPRODUCIBLE 25** and **G-15B**.

TECHNOLOGY TIP

Using an Interactive Whiteboard

If you use an interactive whiteboard, pull up two interactive dice for the lesson. Also scan and pull up the corresponding recording sheet **(REPRODUCIBLE 24)**.

with students that they will be playing the game *Go the Distance*. Explain that the goal of the game is to be as close to ten yards without going over, just like the distance they had been running/jumping. However, rather than running or jumping, they will be rolling dice to determine the distance.

2. Hand two dice (labeled *1–6*) to a student near you. Ask the student to roll the dice and tell the class the two numbers rolled.

3. Ask the class to respond with the sum of the two numbers.

4. Show students the *Go the Distance* Recording Sheet, Customary Version (REPRODUCIBLE 24). Point out that students have the option to record the sum of the dice in either inches or feet. Which one should they pick?

5. Share with students that the goal of the game is, after ten rounds, to have a sum as close to 10 yards (thirty feet) without going over. Say, "Just like in a football game, you want to get ten yards. But in this game, you get ten chances, not just four. Deciding whether to record your sum in inches or feet will be important in helping you reach this goal."

6. Have students collectively determine if the number generated should be inches or feet and record it on the recording sheet.

7. Now pass the pair of dice to another student. The student rolls the dice and reads the two numbers rolled out loud. The class responds with the sum of the numbers and decides collectively whether it should be recorded in inches or feet. Record the sum accordingly.

8. Repeat Step 7 until the recording sheet is full (ten rounds). When the inches add up to

more than a foot, teach students how to condense and record this as feet plus inches in the Running Total column of the recording sheet. This is an example from a classroom during the modeling portion of the lesson:

Roll	Inches	Feet	Running Total
1		5	5 feet
2	11		5 feet 11 inches
3		4	9 feet 11 inches
4		9	18 feet 11 inches
5		7	25 feet 11 inches
6	6		26 feet 5 inches
7			

In this example, when students rolled a 6 in Round 6, the choice between inches and feet was easy—if they had assigned the value of 6 to feet, they would have gone over 30 feet (10 yards). At this point in the game it's appropriate to review how to change 12 inches into 1 foot.

9. Once all ten rounds have been played, complete the last step of the game, which is computing how far away the final entry in the Running Total column is from 10 yards. This will require multiple ways of thinking, as some students will wish to count up while others will use subtraction and yet others may have a different method.

TEACHING TIP
The Importance of Practice
Some students will want to offer their reasoning as to why they choose inches or feet. Refrain from discussing skill or strategies during the teaching part of the lesson. The purpose is to give students as much practice as possible first; they will then have the opportunity to come back later and discuss their experiences after they have played the game independently over a period of time. That being said, students tend to approach this game multiple ways. Two common strategies are:

- if a larger sum is rolled, students assign it inches and when a smaller sum is rolled, assign it feet; and

- students assign all sums feet until getting close to 25–28 feet and then they assign inches for the remaining rolls.

TEACHING TIP
Changing 12 Inches to 1 Foot
To help visual learners see how 12 inches becomes a foot, have rulers available. Convert not only 12 inches to 1 foot, but try more than 12 inches, hence teaching students what to do with the "leftover" inches (for example, 13 inches would be 1 foot and 1 inch). Students can also touch and count on from the starting number of inches.

TEACHING TIPS
Pairing Students

When pairing students for this game, consider placing students of similar ability together. Like ability ensures the mathematical engagement of both students. One student, for example, won't be making all the decisions for the game because of their strength in number sense and computation while the other becomes a bystander. However, after students have had experience in playing the game numerous times on numerous occasions, partnering them with someone who has different thinking provides students with an opportunity to grow in their mathematical understandings.

Emphasize Collaboration

For Part III, "Active Engagement," students should test the game out with their partner, not play against him or her. The goal is for students to work together in understanding how to play the game and the math that is involved. When students have the opportunity to play the game independently (Part IV), they can play each other.

A CHILD'S MIND
Making Math Memorable

You might choose to share the universal symbols for inches (″) and feet (′) with students. To do this, encourage movement. Have students stand on two legs for inches and one leg for feet; raise two hands for inches and only one for feet; hold up two index fingers for inches and only one for feet, and so on. Connecting movement to math engages the kinesthetic learner and aids in memory retention.

Part III: Active Engagement

Engage students to ensure they understand how to play the game.

10. Now give students the opportunity to explore the game in pairs. Each pair should determine a playing space (desk or table) and have two dice (labeled *1–6*), two pencils, and two copies of the *Go the Distance* Recording Sheet, Customary Version (REPRODUCIBLE 24). You may also choose to have rulers available for each student.

11. As students are playing, circulate. Clarify misunderstandings and confirm correct play. Ask questions to check students' understanding (see "Key Questions," page 83). Note that it is okay for students to have an underdeveloped concept of "getting close to, without going over, 10 yards" at this time.

Part IV: The Link

Students play the game independently.

12. Set students up for independent practice with the game. If students don't already have the directions, distribute the *Go the Distance* Game Directions (REPRODUCIBLE G-15A).

13. Designate and share a storage area for the *Go the Distance* materials. This encourages students to be self-sufficient in gathering the materials whenever there is time allotted to independently play the game.

MATH WORKSHOP AND SUMMARIZING THE EXPERIENCE

Teach this game at the beginning of the week to the whole class, then make it an integral part of your math workshop (for more on math workshop, see *Math Workshop* by Jennifer Lempp). Collect students' recording sheets each time they play. To wrap up the game or to encourage friendly competition, create a "Class Leader Board." Students add their winning totals to the board, highlighting how close they can get to 10 yards. Come together later in the week to reflect on the game. Connect students' learning to number and operations and discuss some of the strategies (the addition and subtraction thinking) that students practiced.

DIFFERENTIATING YOUR INSTRUCTION

Going Over

Up to this point, students have been instructed to get as close to 10 yards without going over. Increase the challenge of the game by allowing students to go over, but still remain as close to 10 yards as possible. This gets students thinking about positive and negative numbers and encourages additional strategy in playing the game. This challenge can also be done with the metric version of the game.

Have to Halve
(A Game of Partitioning)

Recommended Grades 1–3

Time Instruction: 45–60 minutes
Independent Play: 20–30 minutes

TEACHING TIP
Quiet Dice
Rolling dice can create a lot of noise. To lessen the noise, use foam dice or pad students' workspaces with foam or fabric placemats.

TIME SAVER
Managing Materials
For ease in managing the distribution of materials, place one die and enough geo bands or rubber bands for a group of four students (approximately 50 rubber bands) in quart-size sandwich bags.

Overview
Each player has a geoboard and begins by placing one large geo or rubber band around the perimeter of their geoboard to create a square. Players then take turns rolling a die to determine their next move. If a player rolls an even number, they must partition the largest section remaining in half (in the case of the first turn, this would mean partitioning the square in half) on their geoboard. If a player rolls an odd number, additional rules apply. The winner of the game is the first player to partition all the halves into half on their geoboard, creating sixteen equal parts.

Materials
- geoboard (standard 25-pegged), 1 per player
- dice (labeled *1–6*)
- geo bands or large rubber bands, approximately 12 per player
- *Have to Halve* Game Directions (**REPRODUCIBLE G-16**), 1 per group of 2–4 students

Related Game
Game 1: Anything but Nothing! (Partitioning Shapes)

Key Questions
- What is one way you might partition this square into two equal halves? Is there another way? Show me.
- Can equal shares of identical wholes have different shapes? How do you know?

- How would you describe this portion of the whole? (Grade 2)
- What is the area of this fraction part of the whole? (Grade 3)

Teaching Directions
Part I: The Connection
Relate the game to students' ongoing work.

Connect the lesson to previous content. If students have been working with identifying shapes, tell them, "We have been discussing shapes and identifying them. Today we will be working on partitioning a special rectangle, a square, into halves."

Part II: The Teaching
Introduce and model the game to students.

1. Gather students together on the floor. Give each student a geoboard and approximately 12 geo bands or rubber bands.

2. If students have not used a geoboard or could benefit from a review of it, provide a couple of minutes of exploration time with the geoboards. Note that for this game, the square-pegged side of a geoboard will be used, not the circular-pegged side.

3. Let students know they will be playing the game *Have to Halve*. The game board is their geoboard. To start each game, a band needs to be wrapped around the outside of their board to form the largest square possible. Show students how to wrap a geo band (or rubber band) around the outside pegs of their geoboards to form a square. Have students do this on their own geoboards (they'll need to use a large-size band). Emphasize the appropriate use of bands—bands should only be used on the geoboards—definitely not to sling at other students!

LEARNING TARGETS
Post the game's Learning Targets for students to see. This helps reinforce what students are responsible for learning as they play the game.

Grade 1:
- I can partition rectangles into two and four equal shares.
- I can describe the shares using the words *halves, fourths,* and *quarters.*

Grade 2:
- I can partition rectangles into two and four equal shares.
- I can describe the shares using the words *halves, fourths,* and *quarters.*
- I can use the phrase *half of.*
- I understand that equal shares of identical wholes may not have the same shape.

Grade 3:
- I can partition shapes into parts with equal area.
- I can express the area of each part as a fraction of the whole.

TEACHING TIP
Arranging Students
For the modeling part of this game, have students sit in a circle or on the perimeter of a rectangular space such as a rug. Make sure there is ample room in the middle for all students to see the demonstration.

TECHNOLOGY TIP
Using an Interactive Whiteboard
To model this game, you may use an actual geoboard or alternatively use an interactive whiteboard. For the latter, select the geoboard from the math toolkit. Then simply use the markers to demonstrate how to loop the rubber band around the pegs, forming the largest square possible. Yet another option, the National Library of Virtual Manipulatives offers an interactive geoboard on their website, nlvm.usu.edu. You should be able to find the geoboard in the geometry strand of any grade band.

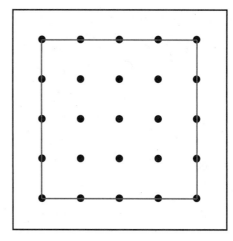

4. After all students have formed a square on their geoboards, explain that in this game, the objective is to partition spaces in half, always starting with the largest space. Demonstrate how to partition the largest square in half using a geo or rubber band:

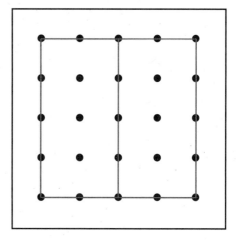

TEACHING TIP
Turn and Talk
Turn and talk is a powerful way to encourage students to share their thinking prior to sharing it with the whole class. For this game, students turn and talk with their neighbor about what they know about partitioning squares. Make a turn and talk brief while also meeting the social needs of students.

5. Have students do the same with their geoboards. Once each student has partitioned the square on their geoboard, say, "There are other ways to partition the square in half. Turn to your neighbor and with your geoboards, explore other ways to divide the large square you begin with in half."

6. After 30 seconds, bring students back together and ask them to share their discoveries out loud. Most students will have discovered that the square on their geoboards can be

divided in half on both diagonals as well as horizontally and vertically through the center.

7. Now proceed with how a partitioning move is determined in the game. Explain to students that players take turns rolling the die; there are four moves determined by the roll of the die:

- *Even number:* If an even number is rolled, the player must partition the largest section on their geoboard in half (point out that this is what students just did).

- *The number 1:* If a 1 is rolled, the player must remove the last band placed on their geoboard. The only exception to this is if the player rolls a 1 on their first roll, in which case they simply skip a turn as there are no bands to remove yet (beyond the starting one around the perimeter, which stays).

- *The number 3:* If a 3 is rolled, the player skips a turn and will have to wait until their next turn to try to make a move.

- *The number 5:* If playing in a group of 3 or 4 and a 5 is rolled, the order of play is reversed, meaning play reverses so if playing in clockwise order play would switch to counter-clockwise if a 5 were rolled. (If playing with only 2 players, this makes no difference and just results in a loss of a turn as if a 3 was rolled.)

8. The best way to review these moves is to get students playing. Have students take turns rolling the die; work together as a class to determine the next move based on the roll. Talk through each move. When an even number is rolled, emphasize the importance of partitioning the largest section on the geoboard; if a smaller section is partitioned, the player must remove the band and give up their turn until next time. Here are some examples of

DIFFERENTIATING YOUR INSTRUCTION

Unique Ways to Partition

Some students may offer more unique ways of dividing the geoboard in half, but for the teaching of the game, it is best to keep to the four ways described in Step 6. However, keep track of those students who offered unique ways to partition. Group those students together when it comes time for independent play of the game and encourage them to continue to think creatively.

TEACHING TIP

Displaying the Four Game Moves

Make sure the four game moves are displayed where everyone can see them. The moves can be abbreviated as follows:

Have to Halve Game Moves

If roll is . . .

    2, 4, 6 = partition the largest section

    1 = remove the last band placed

    3 = loss of turn

    5 = reverse play

what geoboards might look like after two rolls, each generating an even number (partitioning move). Note that the largest section is always the one that has been partitioned each time:

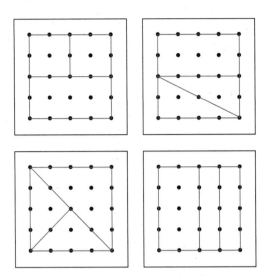

9. As you continue playing the game with students, intentionally make a wrong partitioning move to further emphasize that the largest section must always be partitioned. For example, let's use the first geoboard from the geoboards pictured; a third partitioning move would qualify as any of the following:

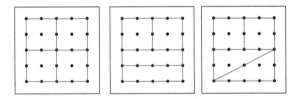

However, a third partitioning move that wouldn't qualify is the following (note that the section partitioned is not the largest section):

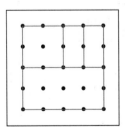

Have students discuss the difference between a qualifying move and a nonqualifying one.

10. Continue modeling the game with students until they have a firm grasp of the procedures and moves. Determine whether students understand the concept of the game by inserting a quick formative assessment such as thumbs-up.

11. Once the majority of students have a firm understanding of the game, reveal how the game is won: the first player to completely partition his or her geoboard—so that there are sixteen equal parts—is the winner.

Part III: Active Engagement

Engage students to ensure they understand how to play the game.

12. Now give students the opportunity to explore the game in groups of 2–4 players. Each student will need a geoboard and approximately 12 geo or rubber bands. Each group will need one die.

13. As students are playing, circulate. Clarify misunderstandings and confirm correct play. Ask questions to check students' understanding (see "Key Questions," page 88).

Part IV: The Link

Students play the game independently.

14. Set students up for independent practice with the game. If students don't already have the directions, distribute the *Have to Halve* Game Directions (REPRODUCIBLE G-16).

15. Designate and share a storage area for the *Have to Halve* materials. This encourages students to be self-sufficient in gathering the materials whenever there is time allotted to independently play the game.

 TEACHING TIPS

Formative Assessment

Formative assessments are necessary to gauge student understanding. They may be used before, during, or after a lesson. In the case of demonstrating this game, a formative assessment is recommended to determine if students are ready to play independently. Consider a quick thumbs-up assessment. Ask students, "Do you feel you understand the game enough to play on your own?" Have students put their thumbs up to indicate, "Yes, I completely understand. I know this," and thumbs down if "No, I need more time. I don't understand all the steps yet." Students may also show a thumbs-out to indicate uncertainty, "I mostly understand; however, I need to see a bit more demonstration." If the majority of students do not respond with a thumbs-up, continue guided teaching of the game.

Providing Choice in Student Grouping

Having students self-select and form their own groups is not always in the best interest of *all* students; however, you can introduce choice when grouping students. To do so, first have students choose a partner and then, as the teacher, "pair up" the pairs to form groups of four. This way you can offer students choice while still managing the groups, making sure there is a balance of personalities and mathematical understanding in each. Also refer back to your observations of those students who offered creative partitioning methods. Consider grouping those students together.

The Importance of Asking Questions

Asking key questions assists you in understanding how or if students are understanding the math. When you ask key questions, students get to hear other students' thinking and further develop their own understanding of the content.

TEACHING TIP
Modeling Productive Independent Play

The best way for students to know what is expected of them when playing independently is to model appropriate behavior. In the case of this game, act out how you want students to get the game materials: select one geoboard and a handful of bands, calmly go to a learning space, and start playing. After pretending to play the game, carefully gather the materials, and quietly return them to their storage area. Once you've demonstrated this, ask student volunteers to model productive independent play. Remember, it is important to never act out or encourage others to act out *unwanted* behavior.

MATH WORKSHOP AND SUMMARIZING THE EXPERIENCE

Teach this game at the beginning of the week to the whole class, then make it an integral part of your math workshop (for more on math workshop, see *Math Workshop* by Jennifer Lempp). Come together later in the week and have students recreate their best round. Then do the classroom sharing method called "Give and Go." Each student walks around the classroom with their work and finds a classmate who is not engaged in a conversation. The students pair up and each "gives" their strategy for playing the game while the other listens. Then the two students "go," meaning they find another solo classmate and start Give and Go again. Typically five minutes is enough time for this way of summarizing and sharing ideas.

ASSESSMENT

After students have had multiple opportunities to practice the game independently, use the *Have to Halve* Assessment (**REPRODUCIBLE 26**) to further check for their understanding.

Line Plot Tic-Tac-Toe

Overview

This game is similar to the classic game of tic-tac-toe, with a line plot serving as the game board. Players take turns rolling a die to determine where they place an X on the line plot. Each time a player rolls the die, they have a choice of either:

- playing to win: placing an X on the line plot, above the corresponding number, or

- playing to block: erasing their opponent's X, if there is one above the corresponding number.

The first player to have three consecutive Xs in their color above a number on the line plot wins.

Materials

- rulers, 1 per student

- colored pencils (with erasers or an eraser to share), each a different color, 2 per pair of students

- dice (labeled *1–6*), 1 per pair of students

- *Line Plot Tic-Tac-Toe* Game Board (REPRODUCIBLE 27), 1 per pair of students

- *Line Plot Tic-Tac-Toe* Game Directions (REPRODUCIBLE G-17), 1 per pair of students

Related Games

Game 8: Compare (Measurement Version)

Game 11: Coordinate Tic-Tac-Toe

Game 15: Go the Distance (Customary and Metric Versions)

Recommended Grade 2

Time Instruction: 45–60 minutes
Independent Play: 20–30 minutes

TIME SAVER
Reusable or Make-Your-Own Game Boards

There are several options for creating game boards for *Line Plot Tic-Tac-Toe*. You may use the reproducible provided, making consumable copies, 1 per pair of students. For reusable copies, laminate a set of game boards or place them in plastic sleeves and provide dry erase markers instead of colored pencils. Alternatively, have students draw their own line plot to use as a game board, either on paper or individual whiteboards. Some options (such as paper) are better than others if you want to keep a running record of students' work.

TEACHING TIP
Quiet Dice
Rolling dice can create a lot of noise. To lessen the noise, use foam dice or pad students' workspaces with foam or fabric placemats.

LEARNING TARGET

Post the game's Learning Target for students to see. This helps reinforce what students are responsible for learning as they play the game.

Grade 2:

- I can represent data by creating a line plot where the horizontal scale is marked off in whole-number units.

Key Questions

- What is a line plot? Why do we use line plots?

- If you roll a one [or two, three, four, five, six], what move might you make next? Why?

- Should you play to win or play to block? Why?

- What object in real life might be similar in length (centimeters, inches, or feet) to this number (point to a number on the line plot)?

Teaching Directions

Part I: The Connection

Relate the game to students' ongoing work.

Revisit some of the measurement activities students have been participating in thus far. Discuss what students have learned and know about measurement. Have students take out their pencils and, using rulers, measure and record the lengths of their pencils in centimeters. Then have them turn to a partner to check the accuracy of their measurements. Tell students that today they are going to learn how to represent this data on a line plot.

Part II: The Teaching

Introduce and model the game to students.

1. To prepare for this game, first introduce students to a line plot. Draw a line plot on the board, large enough for all students to see. Label the line plot, starting with the number 4 and ending with the number 19. These numbers correspond to the shortest and longest lengths of a pencil (the shortest a pencil with an eraser can typically be to still get sharpened is 4 centimeters, whereas an unsharpened pencil with an eraser is 19 centimeters—the longest it could be). Your line plot should look something like the one shown next to this step.

2. Next, model how to mark the line plot. Tell students that the length of your pencil is 13

4 5 6 7 8 9 10 11 12 13 14 15 16 17 18 19

centimeters. Place an X above the 13 on the line plot.

3. Invite students to place an X above the number on the line plot that represents the length of their pencil. Take time to emphasize the importance of the X being similar in size and stacked on top of the previous X when the piece of data (in this case the length of the pencil in centimeters) is the same as one previously plotted. The line plot might look like this after several contributions:

4. Once every student has had an opportunity to mark their pencil measurements on the line plot, point out where three pieces of data occur on a number. In the example given, highlight the numbers 13, 14, and 17, as these numbers each have three Xs above them.

5. Next tell students they will be playing the game *Line Plot Tic-Tac-Toe*. Explain that in this game, they will be rolling a die to generate the data for the line plot. Say, "Each player will roll a die and mark the number rolled with an X on the line plot. Each player will have a different-color pencil, so you will easily be able to differentiate whose piece of data is placed on the line plot."

6. Since a die needs to be rolled, ask students to gather around a table or space on the floor.

7. Display an enlarged line plot in the middle of the demonstration area (this can be a copy of the *Line Plot Tic-Tac-Toe* Game Board (REPRODUCIBLE 27) or a drawing of your own line plot on a poster-size piece of paper). Make sure the line plot is labeled, starting with the number 1 and ending with the number 6.

8. Give students a few rounds of practice simply rolling the die and marking the corresponding number on the line plot with a clear X.

TEACHING TIP
Line Plots: Teaching Slowly and Deliberately
Line plots help you compare data. For young students it's important to emphasize precision and accuracy in marking line plots. Use clear language and demonstrate as much as needed when encouraging students to add their data to a line plot.

TEACHING TIP
Arranging Students
For the modeling part of this game, have students make two concentric circles. In the first circle, students kneel or sit; in the second, students stand. This ensures that everyone can view the demonstration area.

TECHNOLOGY TIP
Using an Interactive Whiteboard
To model this game, you may either gather students around a demonstration area and display the game board on paper or alternatively use an interactive whiteboard. For the latter, select an interactive die from the tool kit. Create a line plot using a pen at the bottom of the screen. Use this and two differing colors of pens or stamps to demonstrate the game.

9. Once students are comfortable plotting the numbers generated from a roll of the die, introduce the two main motives of the game. Relate the motives to the traditional tic-tac-toe, "Just like the game of tic-tac-toe, there are two motives for the moves you make— playing to win and playing to block. In the traditional tic-tac-toe, a game is won when a player has three of their markers in a row, vertically, horizontally, or diagonally. In *Line Plot Tic-Tac-Toe*, you win by getting three same-color Xs stacked on a number in the line plot." Share with students that each time you roll, you have a choice of either:

- *playing to win:* placing an X on the line plot, above the corresponding number, or

- *playing to block:* erasing your opponent's X, if there is one above the corresponding number.

10. Demonstrate the choices. Roll the die. Place an X above the corresponding number on the line plot. Ask a student to do the same, rolling the die and placing an X (in a different color) above the corresponding number on the line plot. Continue alternating turns until there's an opportunity to place an X or erase an X. Think out loud about what to do—should you play to win or play to block?

11. In the following example game, after a few alternating plays of teacher versus students, the number 3 was rolled multiple times, twice for the teacher (who is using blue) and once for the students (who are using the color black). By placing their X on 3, the students blocked the teacher from making three consecutive Xs.

TEACHING TIP
The Importance of Practice
Some students will want to offer their reasoning as to why they choose to write or erase an X. Other students may not fully understand why sometimes they would erase an X and other times just stack their X on top of their opponent's. Regardless, refrain from discussing strategy, skill, and luck at this time. Wait until all students have had many days of practice with the game before engaging in this conversation.

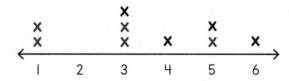

12. Continue modeling the game with students until they have a firm grasp of the procedures and moves. Determine whether students understand the concept of the game by inserting a quick formative assessment such as thumbs-up.

Part III: Active Engagement

Engage students to ensure they understand how to play the game.

13. Now give students the opportunity to explore the game in pairs. Each pair of students will need two different-color pencils, a die (labeled *1–6*), and a line plot (either the line plot from **REPRODUCIBLE 27** or have students draw their own line plot on a piece of paper).

14. As students are playing, circulate. Clarify misunderstandings and confirm correct play. Ask questions to check students' understanding (see "Key Questions," page 96).

15. Students will likely finish at various times. You may wish to have them all play for a certain amount of time or a certain number or rounds. Whatever is decided, it is important that students know the time frame and expectations.

Part IV: The Link

Students play the game independently.

16. Set students up for independent practice with the game. If students don't already have the directions, distribute the *Line Plot Tic-Tac-Toe* Game Directions (**REPRODUCIBLE G-17**).

17. Designate and share a storage area for the *Line Plot Tic-Tac-Toe* materials. This encourages students to be self-sufficient in gathering the materials whenever there is time allotted to independently play the game.

TEACHING TIPS

Formative Assessment

Formative assessments are necessary to gauge student understanding. They may be used before, during, or after a lesson. In the case of demonstrating this game, a formative assessment is recommended to determine if students are ready to play independently. Consider a quick thumbs-up assessment. Ask students, "Do you feel you understand the game enough to play on your own?" Have students put their thumbs up to indicate, "Yes, I completely understand. I know this," and thumbs down if "No, I need more time. I don't understand all the steps yet." Students may also show a thumbs-out to indicate uncertainty, "I mostly understand; however, I need to see a bit more demonstration." If the majority of students do not respond with a thumbs-up, continue guided teaching of the game.

Pairing Students

For the modeling part of this game, pair students who have different levels of understanding of plotting data on a line plot. This helps students learn the procedures of the game. Once students have been introduced to the game and have an understanding of the procedural side of it, then pair students who have similar abilities.

TEACHING TIP
Play It at Home!

The game *Line Plot Tic-Tac-Toe* can be played easily at home. For home use, *Line Plot Tic-Tac-Toe* needs only a dice (labeled 1–6), paper (for the line plot), and colored pencils. Send home copies of the *Line Plot Tic-Tac-Toe* Game Directions **(REPRODUCIBLE G-17)** as necessary.

MATH WORKSHOP AND SUMMARIZING THE EXPERIENCE

Teach this game at the beginning of the week to the whole class, then make it an integral part of your math workshop (for more on math workshop, see *Math Workshop* by Jennifer Lempp). Come together later in the week and hold a whole-class discussion around students' learning. Invite students to share the strategies they used for determining their moves in the game. Ask them if skill, luck, or both were involved in the game and to explain their position.

As part of summarizing the experience, do a *Take a Stand* activity. Ask students a yes-or-no question. You might say, "I think skill played more of a role in this game." Or "A dry erase marker is approximately five inches." Without speaking, students move to the back of the room if they agree, the front of the room if they disagree, or somewhere in the middle of the room if they feel the answer is neither yes or no but both. Movement is a great way to help make math memorable!

March to the Meter

Overview

This game provides practice not only in measurement but in number and operations as students practice counting on and starting at numbers other than zero. Students, playing in pairs, use two different-color game markers to "march" to the end of the meter stick. Each player rolls two dice, adds up the rolled numbers, and makes a move up the meter stick in centimeters, equivalent to the sum. Play alternates. The player who gets to the end of the meter stick (100 centimeters) or beyond first is the winner.

Materials

- meter sticks, 1 per pair of students
- game markers (chips, tiles, pawns, etc.), each a different color, 2 per pair of students
- dice (labeled *1–6*), 2 per pair of students
- *March to the Meter* Recording Sheet (REPRODUCIBLE 28), 1 per pair of students
- *March to the Meter* Game Directions (REPRODUCIBLE G-18), 1 per pair of students

Related Games

Game 12: Desktop Shuffleboard (A Measurement Game)

Game 15: Go the Distance (Customary and Metric Versions)

Recommended Grades K–2

Time Instruction: 45–60 minutes
Independent Play: 15–20 minutes

TIME SAVER
Managing Materials
To manage materials for this game, keep the game markers and dice in quart-size sandwich bags and the game directions in student binders or folders. Also consider making additional copies of the directions and posting them throughout the classroom for students to refer to during independent play.

TEACHING TIPS
Don't Have Enough Dice?
If you do not have enough dice for two per pair of students, use spinners sectioned 1–6.

Quiet Dice
Rolling dice can create a lot of noise. To lessen the noise, use foam dice or pad students' workspaces with foam or fabric placemats.

LEARNING TARGETS

Post the game's Learning Targets for students to see. This helps reinforce what students are responsible for learning as they play the game.

Grade K:
· I can compare two lines to see which is "more" or "less" and describe the difference.

Grade 1:
· I can express the length as a whole number of length units.

· I understand that the length measurement of an object is the number of same-size length units that span it with no gaps or overlaps.

Grade 2:
· I can measure the length using a meter stick.

· I can estimate lengths using units of centimeters and meters.

· I can measure to determine how much longer one line is than another.

TEACHING TIP
Arranging Students

For the modeling part of this game, have students make two concentric circles. In the first circle, students kneel or sit; in the second, students stand. This ensures that everyone can view the demonstration area.

Key Questions

• How many units is your marker from the end of the meter stick?

• What is the difference in centimeters between your partner's marker and yours?

• At what place on the meter stick is your marker about halfway to the end? What objects in the classroom might be similar in length?

Teaching Directions
Part I: The Connection
Relate the game to students' ongoing work.

Younger students are excited about learning how tall they are. Gather them around a demonstration area and show them a meter stick. Explain that the meter stick is a valuable measuring tool. Using the stick, show how small they likely were when they were born. Then show how tall they are now—there's quite a difference!

Part II: The Teaching
Introduce and model the game to students.

1. Gather students around a demonstration area, ideally a large table, group of desks pushed together, or the floor. While students are assembling, place the meter stick, two dice labeled *1–6*, and two different-color game markers in the middle of the demonstration area.

2. Explain that the meter stick will be the game board for today's game, *March to the Meter*. Place the two game markers at the end of the meter stick where it may be marked with a 0.

3. Begin modeling the game by first rolling the two dice. Have students add up the two numbers rolled; what is the sum?

4. The sum indicates the number of centimeters a player should move their marker up the meter stick. Show this by moving one of the markers on the meter stick.

5. Repeat Steps 3 and 4, only this time moving the other marker up the meter stick.

6. Alternate play, calling on student volunteers to roll the dice and collaborate with their classmates to determine their move.

7. Continue modeling the game with students until they have a firm grasp of the procedures and moves. Determine whether students understand the concept of the game by inserting a quick formative assessment such as thumbs-up.

Part III: Active Engagement
Engage students to ensure they understand how to play the game.

8. Now give students the opportunity to explore the game in pairs. Each pair of students will need a meter stick, two dice labeled *1–6*, and two different-color game markers.

9. As students are playing, circulate. Clarify misunderstandings and confirm correct play. Ask questions to check students' understanding (see "Key Questions," page 102).

10. To further check for student understanding, after the game is up and running and each student has a marker somewhere other than 0 or 100 centimeters on their meter sticks, play a quick round of *Freeze*. Tell students that when you call out "Freeze," all games are "frozen." Students then need to look around the room and identify an object that is approximately the same length as the place their marker is at on their meter stick.

Part IV: The Link
Students play the game independently.

11. Set students up for independent practice with the game. If students don't already have the directions, distribute the *March to the Meter* Game Directions (REPRODUCIBLE G-18).

 TEACHING TIPS
Formative Assessment
Formative assessments are necessary to gauge student understanding. They may be used before, during, or after a lesson. In the case of demonstrating this game, a formative assessment is recommended to determine if students are ready to play independently. Consider a quick thumbs-up assessment. Ask students, "Do you feel you understand the game enough to play on your own?" Have students put their thumbs up to indicate, "Yes, I completely understand. I know this," and thumbs down if "No, I need more time. I don't understand all the steps yet." Students may also show a thumbs-out to indicate uncertainty, "I mostly understand; however, I need to see a bit more demonstration." If the majority of students do not respond with a thumbs-up, continue guided teaching of the game.

Providing Choice in Student Pairs
For this game, allow students to choose their partners or use a random strategy (such as pulling sticks with students' names on them). Regardless of the pairing, students of varying abilities will be able to access the mathematics required to play the game because the game utilizes probability in the rolling of the dice as well as computation skills.

DIFFERENTIATING YOUR INSTRUCTION

Change up the game by having students play the following versions:

March to the 0.5 Meter

Players follow the same procedures as in *March to the Meter*, only the winner is the player who gets to the middle of the meter stick (50 centimeters) first.

Hyper March

Add more dice to be rolled. Playing with three or four dice makes the sums more likely to be greater, therefore resulting in bigger movements up the meter stick.

12. Designate and share a storage area for the *March to the Meter* materials. This encourages students to be self-sufficient in gathering the materials whenever there is time allotted to independently play the game.

13. Also distribute copies of the *March to the Meter* Recording Sheet (REPRODUCIBLE 28). Ask students to record their moves using the recording sheet and complete a sheet for each game they play. Students should hand in their recording sheets as a record of being on task and learning.

MATH WORKSHOP AND SUMMARIZING THE EXPERIENCE

Teach this game at the beginning of the week to the whole class, then make it an integral part of your math workshop (for more on math workshop, see *Math Workshop* by Jennifer Lempp). Come together later in the week and hold a whole-class discussion around students' learning. Share students' completed recording sheets and have them discuss their experiences playing the game. Have students identify objects around the classroom that are similar in size to the number of centimeters the losing player's marker remained on.

ASSESSMENT

After students have had multiple opportunities to practice the game independently, introduce an "assessment station" to your math workshop. In this station, place varying lengths of masking tape on the floor or table. Students have to determine which measuring tool to use, measure each piece of tape twice using different units like centimeters and inches, and then determine how much longer one piece of tape is than another.

Mosaic (An Area Game)

Overview

In the game of *Mosaic*, players, in pairs, take turns rolling dice to generate dimensions for a rectangle. Using colored pencils (a different color per player), they then draw the rectangle on a shared piece of graph paper (the game board). Players begin the game by drawing rectangles in opposite corners of the game board. Thereafter, each time a player draws a rectangle, the rectangle must share a side or partial side with another rectangle of the same color. Eventually, players' rectangles meet near the middle. When no more rectangles can be drawn on the board, players add up the total area of the rectangles in their color. The winner is the player with the largest total area.

Materials

- notecards (4 inches by 6 inches), 1 per pair of students

- tiles (1-inch squares) or orange pattern blocks, 24 per pair of students

- centimeter graph paper, 1 sheet per pair of students

- dice (labeled *1–6*), 2 per pair of students

- colored pencils, each a different color, 2 per pair of students

- *Mosaic* Game Directions (REPRODUCIBLE G-19), 1 per pair of students

Related Games

Game 2: Area Stays the Same

Game 16: Have to Halve

Recommended Grades 3–4

Time Instruction: 45–60 minutes
Independent Play: 20–30 minutes

 TIME SAVER
Managing Materials

To manage materials for this game, place sets of the dice and colored pencils in quart-size sandwich bags and the game directions in student binders or folders. Also consider making additional copies of the directions and posting them throughout the classroom for students to refer to during independent play.

 TEACHING TIPS
Don't Have Enough Dice?

If you do not have enough dice for two per pair of students, use spinners sectioned 1–6.

Quiet Dice

Rolling dice can create a lot of noise. To lessen the noise, use foam dice or pad students' workspaces with foam or fabric placemats.

LEARNING TARGETS

Post the game's Learning Targets for students to see. This helps reinforce what students are responsible for learning as they play the game.

Grade 3:

· I can find the area of a rectangle by using addition.

· I can find the area of a rectangle by multiplying the side lengths.

· I can apply the mathematics properties, associative and distributive, to area.

Grade 4:

· I can apply the area formulas for rectangles in mathematical problems.

TEACHING TIP
Turn and Talk

Consider using turn and talk when discussing the area of the notecards. Ask, "What do you know about the associative property?" Have students turn and talk with their neighbor. It is important to put time constraints on this sharing strategy. Keep this brief while still meeting the social needs of students.

Key Questions

- How did you determine the area of this rectangle?

- Why did you choose to draw your rectangle in that space on the game board?

- What are two ways you can determine area?

- How is additive thinking related to multiplicative thinking?

Teaching Directions
Part I: The Connection

Relate the game to students' ongoing work.

Pair students up and give each pair a 4-by-6-inch notecard and 24 tiles (1-inch squares) or orange pattern blocks. Task students with determining the area of the notecard; tell them they can use the tiles (or orange pattern blocks) to help. Some students will tile just the length and the width of the notecard to determine the area, while others will tile the entire card. Encourage all students to tile the entire area. Once students have determined the area, ask them to look at other pairs' cards. Find two cards that are oriented differently and ask, "How can this four-by-six-inch rectangle have the same area as this six-by-four-inch one?" Once students have shared their thoughts, remind them of the associative property of math (if a definition of the associative property is not already posted in the classroom, post it). Next, weave in the distributive property by pointing out how the side of the notecard with the length of 6 can be renamed 5 + 1 or 3 + 3. Make sure a definition of the distributive property is posted in the classroom.

Tell students that today they will be playing a game called Mosaic. In this game they will be using the metric system to measure area. Bring further meaning to the game by sharing pictures of works of art that are mosaic examples. Because mosaic artistry doesn't always involve square tiles in rows and columns, show examples of both, emphasizing those pieces of art that most reflect what students will be doing in the lesson.

Part II: The Teaching

Introduce and model the game to students.

1. Gather students around a demonstration area, ideally a table, desk, or the floor. While students are assembling, place centimeter graph paper, two dice labeled *1–6*, and two different-color pencils in the middle of the demonstration area.

2. Tell students they will be playing the game *Mosaic* with a partner. First introduce the game board by pointing out the piece of centimeter graph paper in the middle of the demonstration area.

3. Explain that each player will start at opposite (diagonal) corners of the game board. Reference the two different-color pencils. Place one pencil at one corner of the game board and the other at the opposite corner.

4. Share that this is a game of drawing rectangles (ultimately forming a mosaic). Players take turns rolling two dice; the numbers rolled determine the dimensions of the rectangle they need to draw.

5. Model rolling the dice, using the numbers to create the dimensions of a rectangle, and drawing the corresponding rectangle in one of the corners of the game board. For example, if you roll a 3 and a 5, the dimensions of your rectangle would be 3 by 5.

6. Label the rectangle with its length and width by writing inside of it (note that the only time it may be challenging to fit the expression inside the rectangle is when a pair of 1s is rolled).

7. Pass the dice to a student sitting on the opposite side of the game board. Instruct them to roll the dice and draw the corresponding rectangle on their side of the graph paper using the colored pencil placed there. Once

A CHILD'S MIND
Making Math Memorable
Posting definitions on classroom walls is something most every teacher does. While it is tempting to post information on walls prior to students arriving (especially in an attempt to be organized and time efficient), research indicates that this is not as meaningful or brain compatible. Instead, post the definitions (in this case, the associative and distributive properties) with students present. Also have them record their learning in their own words, using pictures as well to represent their thinking.

TEACHING TIP
Arranging Students
For the modeling part of this game, have students make two concentric circles. In the first circle, students kneel or sit; in the second, students stand. This ensures that everyone can view the demonstration area.

the rectangle is drawn, make sure it is also labeled.

8. Have the student pass the dice back to you and roll again. This time, when drawing the next rectangle on the game board, point out that it must have at least one side shared with the previous same-color rectangle. Sometimes this will mean the new rectangle will be longer than the one it is sharing a side with and other times it may be shorter yet still sharing a side. Ask students, "With this in mind, where should I draw my next rectangle?"

9. Draw a second rectangle, making sure the dimensions correspond to your roll and that the rectangle shares a side with the rectangle you've previously drawn.

10. Repeat Steps 7 and 8, having another student use the colored pencil on their side and ensuring the new rectangle shares at least one side with the rectangle previously drawn on their side of the board. Make sure the rectangle is correctly labeled.

11. Now introduce the goal of the game. Say, "In the game of *Mosaic*, just like with mosaic artwork, you want to cover as much of the area of the game board with rectangles as possible. Eventually, your partner's rectangles and yours will meet somewhere near the middle." This is what a game board looked like after three rolls for each player:

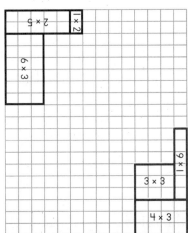

12. Play a few more rounds until students have a firm grasp of the procedures and moves. Determine whether students understand the concept of the game by inserting a quick formative assessment such as thumbs-up.

13. Share how a game ends and a winner is declared: if a player rolls and the corresponding rectangle will no longer fit on the game board, the game is over. Players then add up all of the areas of the rectangles in their color. The player with the greatest total area is the winner.

14. Show students how to add up the area of their rectangles and determine the winner, teacher or students. This is what the example game board looked like after six rounds of play:

TEACHING TIP
Formative Assessment
Formative assessments are necessary to gauge student understanding. They may be used before, during, or after a lesson. In the case of demonstrating this game, a formative assessment is recommended to determine if students are ready to play independently. Consider a quick thumbs-up assessment. Ask students, "Do you feel you understand the game enough to play on your own?" Have students put their thumbs up to indicate, "Yes, I completely understand. I know this," and thumbs down if "No, I need more time. I don't understand all the steps yet." Students may also show a thumbs-out to indicate uncertainty, "I mostly understand; however, I need to see a bit more demonstration." If the majority of students do not respond with a thumbs-up, continue guided teaching of the game.

15. The area of each of the teacher's six rectangles (blue pencil) is 12, 6, 9, 12, 2, 25. The area of each of the students' six rectangles (black pencil) is 10, 2, 18, 12, 15, 9. Players might total their areas as shown on page 106; the example shows the areas of the rectangles, now add space, as numbers strings, to arrive at a total. This work can be done on the back of the graph paper or on a separate paper. Tell students that the small number 2 in the place where an apostrophe might go indicates area (square units).

TEACHING TIP
Computing Area
Students will have multiple approaches for computing the total area in this game. Allow them to use scratch paper, sticky notes, or the back of the game board (graph paper) to write out their thinking. Some students will want the challenge of computing the area in their head and recording that on the game board. Have calculators available to check pencil/paper or mental math.

TEACHING TIP

Adding Up the Rectangle Areas

Most students will choose to use a separate sheet of paper to add up their areas so they don't have to flip the graph paper back and forth. Alternatively, give each player a sticky note to show their work. Then students affix the sticky note to the graph paper and turn both in. As students become more fluent in mental math, they will like the challenge of holding the numbers in their head and recording their total. However, when students don't show their work, it is difficult to determine student errors.

TEACHING TIPS

Providing Choice in Student Grouping

Offer students the choice of working in pairs (two players) or in teams (four players). Most students are aware of their capabilities and will choose the arrangement that meets their needs at the time. Students who are less comfortable with the game procedures may benefit from playing as a team of two against another team of two.

The Importance of Asking Questions

Asking key questions assists you in understanding how or if students are developing strategies. Key questions also prompt students to hear each other's thinking and further develop their own understanding of the content.

Teacher (blue pencil)

$12 + 6 + 9 + 12 + 2 + 25$

$24 + 15 + 2 + 25$

$26 + 40 = 66$ units^2

Students (black pencil)

$10 + 2 + 18 + 12 + 15 + 9$

$10 + 20 + 12 + 24$

$30 + 36 = 66$ units^2

Part III: Active Engagement

Engage students to ensure they understand how to play the game.

16. Now give students the opportunity to explore the game in pairs. Each pair of students will need a sheet of graph paper, two dice (labeled *1–6*), and two different-color pencils.

17. As students are playing, circulate. Clarify misunderstandings and confirm correct play. Ask questions to check students' understanding (see "Key Questions," page 106).

Part IV: The Link

Students play the game independently.

18. Set students up for independent practice with the game. If students don't already have the directions, distribute the *Mosaic* Game Directions (REPRODUCIBLE G-19).

19. Designate and share a storage area for the *Mosaic* materials. This encourages students to be self-sufficient in gathering the materials whenever there is time allotted to independently play the game.

MATH WORKSHOP AND SUMMARIZING THE EXPERIENCE

Teach this game at the beginning of the week to the whole class, then make it an integral part of your math workshop (for more on math workshop, see *Math Workshop* by Jennifer Lempp). After students have had multiple practices with the game of *Mosaic* have them select one of their game boards, to display during a *gallery walk* (see Teaching Tip).

ASSESSMENT

After students have had multiple opportunities to practice the game independently, use the *Mosaic* Assessment (**REPRODUCIBLE 29**) to further check for their understanding.

TEACHING TIP
A Gallery Walk

A *gallery walk* is a way of sharing that allows students to display their work around the room much like artwork is displayed in an art gallery. It provides a nonthreatening way for students to share while also giving them an opportunity to receive feedback from their peers. During a gallery walk, provide sentence starters or questions to help students inquire about each others' work. Sentence starters that work well for this game include:

- How did you decide to place this rectangle here?
- How did you decide which orientation was the best placement?
- Wow, I noticed that . . .
- I like the way you placed . . .

Also consider playing soothing music as students walk around.

Positions
(Identifying and Describing Shapes)

Recommended Grade K

Time Instruction: 30–45 minutes
Independent Play: 15–20 minutes

TEACHING TIPS

A Deck of Cards

For the purpose of this game, a deck of cards consists of 49 cards: two copies each of the first four pages of **REPRODUCIBLE 30** (48 shape cards) and one copy of the star card.

Reusable Cards

To ensure longevity of cards, use thick paper stock and/or laminate them. Store each deck in a quart-size sandwich bag.

TIME SAVER

Coding Cards

Code each set of cards to keep it complete. Ideally, choose to copy each set on a different color of paper to easily differentiate between sets. Alternatively, if using the same color of paper, place a small symbol in the corner of each set's card; use a different symbol for each set so that, if sets become mixed up, you can sort them more easily.

Overview

This game provides students with practice naming shapes and their positions. To set up the game, a star card is placed in the middle of the playing area and four stacks of shape cards are placed faceup around the star in different positions— above, below, in front of, and behind. Students spin a spinner to determine which stack of cards to reference. They then name the shape on the top card of that stack, in addition to its position in relation to the star card. If they are correct, they earn a point and keep the card. The player with the most points (cards) wins.

Materials

- *Positions* Shape Cards (REPRODUCIBLE 30), 1 deck per group of 2–3 students
- *Positions* Spinner (REPRODUCIBLE 31), 1 per group of 2–3 students
- paper clip, 1 per group of 2–3 students
- pencil, 1 per group of 2–3 students
- *Positions* Game Directions (REPRODUCIBLE G-20), 1 per group of 2–3 students

Related Games

Game 7: Compare (Geometry Version)
Game 14: Geometry Go Fish

Key Questions

- When your spinner lands on the option *in front of* (or *above*, *below*, or *behind*), which stack of cards do you go to?

- What is the shape on this card? What words would you use to describe it?

- What are some things in the classroom above you? (ceiling, lights, etc.)

- What are some things below you? (carpeting, tile, etc.)

Teaching Directions

Part I: The Connection

Relate the game to students' ongoing work.

Connect the vocabulary used in this game to students' real life. For example, if students have an assigned order in which they line up when passing through the hallway, discuss who is "in front of" or "behind" them. Also relate the lesson to the hundreds chart. For example, place a chip on number 19 on the chart. Talk about the relative positions of the numbers around 19. Nine is "above." Twenty-nine is "below," 20 is "in front of," and 18 is "behind." Sometimes students will use the phrase "next to," which is fine; however, emphasize that in this game they need to be more specific and instead use phrases like "in front of" and "behind."

Part II: The Teaching

Introduce and model the game to students.

1. Gather students around a demonstration area (table, desk, or floor). Show them the *Positions* Spinner (**REPRODUCIBLE 31**). Explain that they have equal chances to land on one of the four position words (see next page).

LEARNING TARGET

Post the game's Learning Target for students to see. This helps reinforce what students are responsible for learning as they play the game.

Kindergarten:

- I can describe objects using names of shapes and their relative positions.

TECHNOLOGY TIP

Using an Interactive Whiteboard

If an interactive whiteboard is available, a hundreds chart and/or an illustration of students in a line will help launch this lesson. If using a hundreds chart on the interactive whiteboard, simply use the text overlay option to circle the number (in the example, this would be 19).

TEACHING TIP

Arranging Students

For the modeling part of this game, have students make two concentric circles around the demonstration area. In the first circle, students kneel or sit; in the second, students stand. This ensures that everyone can view the demonstration area.

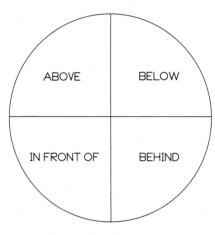

2. Show students the deck of *Positions* Shape Cards (REPRODUCIBLE 30). Find and place the star card face up in the middle of the demonstration area.

3. Next, shuffle and count the remaining cards into four stacks of twelve (for the purposes of introducing the game, four stacks of six will also suffice).

4. Ask students to recount the stacks, making certain stacks have an equal number of cards.

5. Place the four stacks faceup in four different positions relative to the star card in the middle. One stack is above, another below, and the last two on either side of the star card. When done, the setup should look something like this:

TEACHING TIP
Shuffling Cards
Younger students are typically not able to shuffle the cards. If this is the case, demonstrate how to mix the cards with your hands, being careful to keep all the cards facing the same direction (either facedown or faceup).

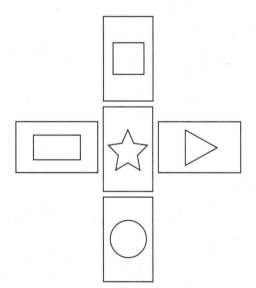

6. At this point in the lesson emphasize how players should arrange themselves around the playing area. Say, "This game is for two or three players. Because the game is practicing relative positions, it is necessary for all players to sit on the same side of the playing area. Sit side by side, next to each other."

7. Invite two or three student volunteers to model the game with you. Arrange them so everyone is sitting on the same side of the playing area.

8. The first student volunteer spins the spinner and announces the outcome; for example, "below." That same student identifies the stack of cards that corresponds with the outcome—in this case the stack of cards below the star card. The student looks at the top card in the stack, names the shape on the card, and reinforces the position. In our example, the student would say something like, "This is a circle and it is below the star," or "The shape below the star is a circle." If the other students playing (or watching in this case) agree, the student earns one point and sets the card aside. If the other players don't agree, they come to a consensus as to who is right; the student ends their turn if they are wrong (no points are gained or lost).

9. Students alternate play, spinning, going to the appropriate stack as directed by the spinner, looking at the top card, and naming the shape, inclusive of its position. If correct, students set the card aside as one point earned.

10. Eventually a player will be looking at the last card in a stack. When this happens, that player earns a bonus point and the game ends. Players then count their cards, each card equating to a game point. The winner is the player with the most points.

TEACHING TIP
Selecting Student Volunteers
Be deliberate about who you select as the student volunteers to demonstrate this game. Select students who are secure in their shape knowledge, because they will be put in a situation in which all of their peers are watching them.

TEACHING TIP
Scoring Variations
As students practice the game of *Positions* independently, adding a scoring variation may be appealing. One variation might be to play three consecutive rounds and add the total number of points from each round. Paper and pencil can be used to keep track of scoring. The winner is always the player with the highest score.

TEACHING TIP
Grouping Students

For Part III, "Active Engagement," group together students who have different levels of understanding of shape and position identification. This approach helps students focus on the procedures for playing the game. After students have been introduced to the game and have an understanding of the steps, pair students with similar ability.

TEACHING TIP
Emphasize Collaboration

For Part III, "Active Engagement," students should test the game out with their group, not playing against each other. The goal is for students to work together in understanding how to play the game and the math that is involved. When students have the opportunity to play the game independently (Part IV), they can play against each other. To support collaborative play at this stage, have students play "against the deck," meaning that once a stack has been depleted, all players count their cards. If the players have more cards than remain in play, they win.

TEACHING TIP
Card Bundling

Younger students sometimes have difficulty managing rubber bands. Consider using plastic baggies or manila envelopes with metal clasps to bundle each deck of cards. If using envelopes, remind students not to seal them but to use the clasp or string.

Part III: Active Engagement
Engage students to ensure they understand how to play the game.

11. Now give students the opportunity to explore the game in groups of two or three. Each group will need a deck of *Positions* Shape Cards (REPRODUCIBLE 30) and a *Positions* Spinner (REPRODUCIBLE 31).

12. As students are playing, circulate. Clarify misunderstandings and confirm correct play. Make sure students are arranging themselves so all players are on the same side of the playing area. This ensures that players are all in the same alignment when using the relative position words. Assist students who are struggling and encourage students to help each other in this first introductory round.

13. Students should play at least one complete round before moving on to Part IV of the lesson. When finished, ask students to arrange their deck of cards in a stack with all cards facing the same way and the star card on top. This makes starting the next round of play easier.

Part IV: The Link
Students play the game independently.

14. Set students up for independent practice with the game. If students don't already have the directions, distribute the *Positions* Game Directions (REPRODUCIBLE G-20).

15. Designate a place in the classroom where the decks of cards can be stored and easily retrieved. Also determine how students will select whom and how many classmates they will play the game with. Let students know that they may play in twos or threes. Emphasize to students, "Be willing to play with different classmates each time you play."

MATH WORKSHOP AND SUMMARIZING THE EXPERIENCE

Teach this game at the beginning of the week to the whole class, then make it an integral part of your math workshop (for more on math workshop, see *Math Workshop* by Jennifer Lempp). Build in time to observe students playing the game. Note their individual skill level; come together later in the week and connect their learning to an analog clock. Ask students questions like:

- Which number on the clock is directly above the hands of the clock?

- Which number on the clock is directly below the hands of the clock?

- Which number is beside . . . ?

- Which number on the clock is next to . . . ?

ASSESSMENT

After students have had multiple opportunities to practice the game independently, use the *Positions* Assessment (**REPRODUCIBLE 32**) to further check their understanding.

TEACHING TIPS

Don't Have an Analog Clock?

If there is no analog clock in the classroom, consider a few options. First, look in the resource room for a traditional yellow analog clock. Second, ask colleagues for one or shop a thrift store for one. Lastly, use **REPRODUCIBLE 33** from Game 21 to make an analog clock or make one using a paper plate and a marker.

An Interactive Whiteboard's Analog Clock

If an interactive whiteboard is available, consider using the analog clock in the tool kit for the summarization of the lesson.

Roll Fives to 60
(An Analog Clock Game)

Recommended Grades 1–3

Time Instruction: 45–60 minutes
Independent Play: 20–30 minutes

TEACHING TIPS

Don't Have an Analog Clock?
If there is no analog clock in the classroom, consider a few options. First, look in the resource room for a traditional yellow analog clock. Second, ask colleagues for one or shop a thrift store for one. Lastly, use **REPRODUCIBLE 33** to make an analog clock or make one using a paper plate and a marker.

An Interactive Whiteboard's Analog Clock
If an interactive whiteboard is available, consider using the analog clock in the tool kit for the summarization of the lesson.

Making Dice Labeled 0–5
There are several options for making the dice required in this game:

- *Relabel existing dice*: Use small, round stickers to relabel existing dice.

- *Write on wooden cubes*: Using a permanent marker, label each face of a wooden cube.

- *Use spinners*: As an alternative to dice, create spinners.

Quiet Dice
Rolling dice can create a lot of noise. To lessen the noise, use foam dice or pad students' workspaces with foam or fabric placemats.

Overview
In this game, the game board is an analog clock. Players take turns rolling two dice labeled *0–5*. When a combination of five is rolled, players snap together five interlocking cubes and place them around the outside circumference of the clock, marking increments of five, starting with the first increment between 12 and 1. The objective is to increase students' understanding that the space between the numerals on an analog clock represent increments of five. The first player or team to snap together twelve sets of five cubes and reach 12 o'clock again is the winner.

Materials
- analog clock
- dice (labeled *0–5*), 2 per group of 2–4 students
- *Roll Fives to 60* Game Board (**REPRODUCIBLE 33**), 1 per student
- interlocking cubes, 60 per student

Related Games
Game 8: Compare (Measurement Version)

Game 15: Go the Distance (Customary and Metric Versions)

Game 18: March to the Meter

Key Questions

- Show me where the half hour is on the clock. How would you write that?

- Show me where the top of the hour is on the clock. How would you write that?

- Where are the five-minute intervals on the clock?

- Count by fives to 60 as you go around the clock face.

- If the minute hand were pointing at the 3, how many minutes past the hour is that? (Substitute numbers 1–6 for this question.)

- If the minute hand were pointing at the 9, how many minutes are there until the next hour? (Substitute the numbers 6–11 for this question.)

Teaching Directions

Part I: The Connection

Relate the game to students' ongoing work.

Ask students to gather in a circle around a demonstration area (table, desk, or floor) and sit crisscross. Place an analog clock in the middle of the area and pour a pile of nickels (play or real coins) into the middle as well. Ask each student to reach in and grab one nickel. Ask, "What is the value of a nickel?" Then count by fives, going around the circle, with a different student calling out the next number in the pattern each time.

Now ask, "How many nickels are in a dollar?" Recount by fives, this time starting with a different student, stopping at the number 100. "How many nickels are needed to get to one hundred?" Count the nickels (students) needed to get to 100. Once students rediscover or confirm that there are 20 fives in 100, gesture to the analog clock and say, "Many of you know there are sixty minutes in an hour. How many fives is that? Let's use our nickels again to find out."

LEARNING TARGETS

Post the game's Learning Targets for students to see. This helps reinforce what students are responsible for learning as they play the game.

Grade 1:
- I can tell and write time in hours and half-hours using analog clocks.

Grade 2:
- I can tell and write time from analog clocks to the nearest five minutes.

Grade 3:
- I can tell and write time to the nearest minute and measure time intervals in minutes.

TEACHING TIP
Creating Order Amid Excitement
Students will be quite excited to see the coins in the middle of the lesson area, especially if the coins are real. Be sure to tell them not to reach in before you have finished dispensing the coins. Then establish an orderly process for how students will each get a coin, such as, "If you have exactly five letters in your first name, reach in and grab a nickel," and "If the same is true about your last name and you have not already done so, reach in and grab just one nickel." An orderly procedure will keep students from bumping heads while simultaneously honoring their excitement.

Count to 60 by fives and then count the number of nickels (students) needed to get to 60.

Have a different set of twelve students count by fives to 60 again, this time placing their nickels around the circumference of the analog clock as they count, aligning each nickel to five-minute increments on the clock. Encourage students to go slowly. Reinforce understanding as needed, "There are twelve fives in sixty. The clock is labeled with the numbers one through twelve. That means there are twelve increments of five around the clock." Collect the nickels at the end of counting.

TEACHING TIP
Analog Versus Digital Clocks
Most classrooms have analog clocks hanging on the wall; regardless, consider doing a compare/contrast with a digital clock (analog and digital clocks are both typically found in secondhand stores). Students not only learn the difference between the two but also understand how time is read on each.

Part II: The Teaching
Introduce and model the game to students.

1. Continue to have students seated around the demonstration area. Revisit the increments of five on a clock, only this time introduce interlocking cubes instead of nickels. Snap five cubes together and place the stick between the 12 and the 1 on the outer circumference of the clock, with the end (not sides) flush to the clock. Say, "In the game today you will be moving around the clock face in increments of five, snapping together cubes to represent your progress."

2. Share the dice (each labeled *0–5*) used in the game. Ask students, "What do you notice about these dice compared to others you've

used before?" Have a discussion about the similarities and differences between these dice and regular dice (typically labeled *1–6*). Students should point out that *Roll Fives to 60*'s dice are different because the dice have numbers rather than dots representing numbers and the numbers are 0–5 not 1–6.

3. Share the *Roll Fives to 60* Game Board (**REPRODUCIBLE 33**). Ask students, "What do you notice about this game board?" They will most likely respond that it looks just like an analog clock. Point out that the 12 is where they will start and finish the game.

4. Now share how a move is made in the game. Players must roll combinations of five to make a move; if they roll something other than a combination of five, say a 1 and a 3, they lose their turn. Ask students, "What combinations of five can be made with the dice?" Do a whole-class share of the possibilities.

5. Once students are familiar with the materials for the game (interlocking cubes, dice, and game board), proceed to modeling the game. Say, "Let's play a round in teams, teacher versus students." Place a second copy of the game board in the middle of the demonstration area, so there is one for each "team."

6. Roll the dice. If a combination of five is rolled, snap together five cubes and place them in the first five-minute increment between 12 and 1 on your game board clock (in order for the sticks to "fit," place each stick so an end is flush to the clock, not a side). If something is rolled other than a combination of five, no move is made (you lose your turn). Pass the dice to the other team (the students).

7. Have a student roll the dice. If a combination of five is rolled, the student snaps together five cubes and places them in the first five-minute increment between 12 and 1 on their game board clock.

TEACHING TIP

Why Does Each Player or Team Need a Game Board?

In *Roll Fives to 60* it is important that each player or team have their own game board. Sharing a game board can result in confusion, as there would be ten interlocking cubes (two sticks of five) at each five-minute increment. Part of the game's objective is to help students understand the increments of five on an analog clock.

8. Play alternates. Students should pass the dice to a different student each time to engage more students.

9. The following is what the game boards looked like in a second-grade classroom after several rounds of play. Students had a firm grasp of the game at this point, indicating to the teacher that it was okay to move on to the "Active Engagement" part of the lesson.

Teacher   Students

TIME SAVER
Managing Materials
For ease in managing the distribution of materials, place the required 120 interlocking cubes in a container (one container for each pair of students playing the game). Then place the two dice (labeled 0–5) in a sandwich bag and include in each container.

Part III: Active Engagement
Engage students to ensure they understand how to play the game.

10. Now give students the opportunity to explore the game in pairs. Each pair will need two dice (labeled *0–5*), two *Roll Fives to 60* Game Boards (REPRODUCIBLE 33) and 120 interlocking cubes, 60 each.

11. As students are playing, circulate. Clarify misunderstandings and confirm correct play. Ask questions to check students' understanding (see "Key Questions," page 119).

12. Allow play to continue until students have completed at least one round.

Part IV: The Link
Students play the game independently.

13. Set students up for independent practice with the game. If students don't already have the directions, distribute the *Roll Fives to 60* Game Directions (REPRODUCIBLE G-21).

14. Designate and share a storage area for the *Roll Fives to 60* materials. This encourages students to be self-sufficient in gathering the materials whenever there is time allotted to independently play the game.

> ### MATH WORKSHOP AND SUMMARIZING THE EXPERIENCE
> Teach this game at the beginning of the week to the whole class, then make it an integral part of your math workshop (for more on math workshop, see *Math Workshop* by Jennifer Lempp). Come together later in the week and have students label an analog clock as a class. Use small sticky notes to mark the clock's increments of 5, 10, and 15. This makes for a nice visual in addition to being a helpful summary of students' learning.

DIFFERENTIATING YOUR INSTRUCTION

Missing Analog Clock Numbers
During Part IV, "The Link," you might want to offer a more challenging version of the game to some students. To do so, use the *Roll Fives to 60* Extension Game Board (REPRODUCIBLE 34). On this game board, the numbers on the analog clock are absent. As students make their way around the clock, they fill in the numbers, recording both the hour and the number of minutes past the hour (in five-minute increments). This extension can also double as an assessment once students have had multiple opportunities playing the game.

Sunshine (A Yahtzee-Like Game)

Recommended Grade 4

Time Instruction: 45–60 minutes
Independent Play: 20–30 minutes

TEACHING TIPS

Making the Dice

There are several options for making the dice required in this game:

- *Relabel existing dice*: Use small, round stickers to relabel existing dice.

- *Write on wooden cubes*: Using a permanent marker, label each face of a wooden cube.

- *Use spinners*: As an alternative to dice, create spinners.

The six faces of each die should show the following:

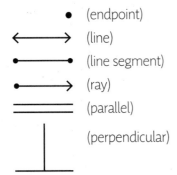

Quiet Dice

Rolling dice can create a lot of noise. To lessen the noise, pad students' desktops with foam or fabric placemats or encourage students to play on a carpet square or carpeted area of the classroom, if available. Also use paper cups instead of plastic cups (the latter make more noise when being used to roll dice).

Overview

This Yahtzee-like game encourages students to improve their understanding of *endpoints*, *lines*, *line segments*, *rays*, *parallel lines*, and *perpendicular lines*. The goal of the game is to get as many points as possible by rolling like symbols according to the score sheet. Only one row of the score sheet can be filled in on each turn, with each turn consisting of rolling the symbol dice up to three times. The player with the most points at the end of ten turns is the winner. Strategy, skill, logic, and luck are all woven into this exciting game.

Materials

- dice (each face with a different symbol— point, line, line segment, ray, parallel lines, and perpendicular lines), 5 per group of 2–4 students

- plastic or paper cup, 1 per group of 2–4 students

- *Sunshine* Score Sheet (REPRODUCIBLE 35), 1 per student (note: the reproducible contains 2 score sheets)

- pencil, 1 per student

- *Sunshine* Game Directions (REPRODUCIBLE G-22), 1 per group of 2–4 students

Related Games

Game 4: Boxed In (A Game of Parallel and Perpendicular Moves)

Game 6: Claim the Dots (Classifying Angles and Lines)

Key Questions

- What is the difference between a line and a line segment?

- What do a line, line segment, and ray all have in common?

- What makes two lines parallel?

- What makes two lines perpendicular?

- What move are you aiming for on the score sheet? Why?

Teaching Directions

Part I: The Connection

Relate the game to students' ongoing work.

Do a quick review of the geometry terms *point, line, line segment, ray, parallel,* and *perpendicular*. Have students use their bodies to help them remember the definitions:

- *Point* can be represented by placing your hand over your fist to form a ball or point.

- *Line* (a straight set of points that extends in both directions without ending) is created by extending each arm out, parallel to the floor, hands open.

- *Line segment* (a part of a line between two endpoints) is similar to *line* above; however, form both hands into fists.

- *Ray* (a part of a line with one endpoint, the other extending in one direction without ending) is also expressed in the same way as *line*, but with one hand balled into a fist and the other hand open.

- *Parallel* is created by extending both arms in front of your body.

- *Perpendicular* is expressed by extending both arms in front of your body and bending one arm 90 degrees up from the elbow, touching both elbows.

LEARNING TARGETS

Post the game's Learning Targets for students to see. This helps reinforce what students are responsible for learning as they play the game.

Grade 4:

- I can identify and draw points, lines, line segments, rays, perpendicular lines, and parallel lines.

- I can identify the above in two-dimensional figures.

A CHILD'S MIND

Making Math Memorable

Having students use motion engages the bodily kinesthetic learning style as well as the episodic memory. Utilizing both help with retention of knowledge.

Part II: The Teaching

Introduce and model the game to students.

1. Gather students around a demonstration area (table, desk, or floor). Show them the dice that will be used in the game *Sunshine*. Distribute the five dice for students to inspect and pass along to another classmate. Ask, "What is different about these dice compared to other dice you've used?" Students will likely point out that these dice have geometry symbols on them rather than dots or numbers.

2. Draw the symbols that appear on the dice on the board, large enough for all students to see. Ask students, "What does each symbol stand for?" Record students' correct responses next to the symbols.

3. Now share with students that they will be rolling not just one or two dice but five (!) dice in this game. To make it easier to roll this many dice, a cup is used. Demonstrate this by placing the five dice into a cup, shaking the cup briefly, and spilling the dice out. Be deliberate in your demonstration; emphasize that the dice should be calmly and carefully spilled out of the cup onto the playing surface.

4. Distribute a copy of the *Sunshine* Score Sheet (REPRODUCIBLE 35) to each student. At the same time make sure each student has a pencil.

5. Unless students are familiar with the game *Yahtzee*, it will likely take some time to carefully explain the use of the score sheet. Start by sharing the objective of the game. Say, "The goal of the game is to get as many points as possible by filling in rows of the score sheet. The numbers 1, 2, 3, 4, and 5 at the top of the score sheet are referring to the five dice. Only one row can be filled in on each turn, so you'll have to decide which row to go for on each turn." Make sure students are clear on "one row"—to check, have each student point to a row and move their finger across it, left to right.

Sunshine Score Sheet

	1	2	3	4	5	total
point						
line						
line segment						
ray						
parallel						
perpendicular						
Total of the top portion:						
*If total for top portion is over 18, add 10 points.						
3 of a kind	Add 10 points.					
4 of a kind	Add 15 points.					
2 parallel & 2 perpendicular	Add 20 points.					
5 rays "SUNSHINE"	Add 25 points.					
Total of the bottom portion:						

6. Share the final rule, "There's one more rule that will help you: on each turn, you have the option of rolling the dice as many as three times. On each roll, you can set aside the dice that have generated symbols you want to keep and try again with the remaining dice."

7. Now have students turn and talk about their score sheets. What do they notice about each of the rows? What has to be rolled to complete each row?

8. Model how the rows are intended to be filled out, starting with the top half. Say, "Let's pretend I am going to try to fill out the second row of my sheet, the *line* row. When it's my turn, I roll the five dice. For purposes of this demonstration, I'm going to pretend that in this roll my dice landed as follows." Set up the five dice so the following faces are up:

9. Have students call out the symbols on the five dice. Remind students, "I want to fill out the *line* row on my score sheet, so which dice do I keep?" It makes sense to keep the two dice that landed with the line symbol facing up:

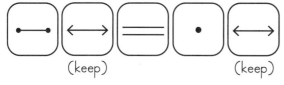

10. Set the two dice that landed with the line symbol facing up to the side of your playing area. Return the other three dice to the cup and roll again. This time pretend your roll generated the following, and set the dice up accordingly:

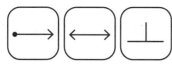

11. Now ask students, "Will any of the dice in this roll help me get closer to filling out the line

row of my score sheet?" Students should pick the second die to keep, as it landed with the line symbol faceup.

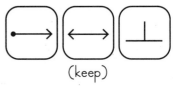

(keep)

12. Set that die aside with the other two dice, so you have three dice with the line symbol. Point out that you now have enough dice not only to fill in the "line" row, but also the "3 of a kind" row on the bottom half of your score sheet. Remind students they still have one more roll left. Return the remaining two dice to the cup.

13. On your third roll, pretend the dice generated the following (set the two dice up accordingly):

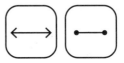

14. Ask students, "Does it make sense to keep these rolls? Why or why not?" Allow a brief discussion. Students should agree on keeping the first die as it is a line symbol. Since three rolls have transpired, your turn is finished, and your play must now be recorded.

15. Model how students should record their play on the top portion of the sheet. This is done by marking each box with the corresponding symbol and counting 1 point per box filled. For this play, four line symbols were generated, so four of the boxes in the line row would be marked and the number 4 written in the Total column:

	1	2	3	4	5	total
point						
line	↙	↙	↙	↙		4
line segment						

16. Play a few more rounds as needed to get students comfortable with the "three rolls a turn" rule and the idea of aiming to fill out one specific row of the score sheet each turn.

17. Once students are comfortable with the top half of the score sheet, introduce the bottom half. As students have noticed, it is slightly different than the top half, though the same rules apply: students must fill out just one row per turn, only these rows request different information. In the example on the previous page, point out that you could've filled out the "3 of a kind row" and stopped after your second roll, or filled out the "4 of a kind row" after your third roll. Emphasize that it's up to the player what row they wish to fill out (top or bottom) with each turn, and to keep in mind that ultimately, they want to gain as many points as possible in the ten turns they get. The following is an example of four of a kind; four of the dice landed with the line side face up.

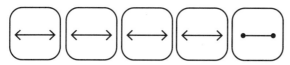

18. Finally, explain that when students fill in one of the rows, they cannot add to or change what they recorded. If they roll something that applies to a row that has already been filled in or applies to no rows, they must record a 0 in one of the yet-to-be-filled rows of their choosing on their recording sheet. This means with each turn the player has the opportunity to reroll the dice three times, setting aside the category they are aiming for. If it doesn't work out, they must still record something in a category on the score sheet and sometimes that may be a zero.

19. Play a few more rounds, now utilizing the entire score sheet, top and bottom. Emphasize that on each turn, up to three rolls can be had.

TEACHING TIP
Formative Assessment

Formative assessments are necessary to gauge student understanding. They may be used before, during, or after a lesson. In the case of demonstrating this game, a formative assessment is recommended to determine if students are ready to play independently. Consider a quick thumbs-up assessment. Ask students, "Do you feel you understand the game enough to play on your own?" Have students put their thumbs up to indicate, "Yes, I completely understand. I know this," and thumbs down if "No, I need more time. I don't understand all the steps yet." Students may also show a thumbs-out to indicate uncertainty, "I mostly understand; however, I need to see a bit more demonstration." If the majority of students do not respond with a thumbs-up, continue guided teaching of the game.

Grouping Students

When pairing students in teams for this game, consider placing students of similar abilities together to ensure both students are engaged. One student, for example, wouldn't be making all the decisions for the game, while the other becomes a bystander. However, after students have had experience in playing the game numerous times on numerous occasions, partnering them with someone who has *different* thinking provides students with an opportunity to grow in their mathematical understandings.

After the first roll of each turn, invite students to think, "With the current roll in mind, are there any rows on the score sheet that we are close to attaining?" Students may have differing ideas about what to "go for." Remind students that they get to return as many dice as they choose to the cup and roll again; this may help with gaining a consensus; however, be prepared to facilitate the decision.

20. A game is ten turns for each player; when ten turns have been had (meaning all ten rows on each player's recording sheet are filled in, even if this means some rows have 0), review how to tally up the final scores and determine a winner, completing the statements at the bottom of the score sheet. Determine whether students understand the concept of the game by inserting a quick formative assessment such as thumbs-up.

21. If students have not already asked, share that the game is called Sunshine for a reason. Say, "If on any turn you attain five dice that are rays, you exclaim, 'Sunshine!' because they are like the rays of the sun. You don't have to roll all five at once, but you have up to three rolls to get five rays. Sunshine gets you the most points." Have students locate the Sunshine row on their score sheets.

Part III: Active Engagement
Engage students to ensure they understand how to play the game.

22. Now give students the opportunity to explore the game in groups of four (for the introduction of the game, playing in groups of four—two teams of two—seems to work well). Each group needs five dice, a cup, and a copy of the *Sunshine* Game Directions (REPRODUCIBLE G-22). Each team needs a copy of the *Sunshine* Score Sheet (REPRODUCIBLE 35 offers two score sheets) and a pencil.

23. As students are playing, circulate. Clarify misunderstandings and confirm correct play. Ask questions to check students' understanding (see "Key Questions," page 125). Have students play at least one game.

Part IV: The Link

Students play the game independently.

24. Set students up for independent practice with the game. This time, you might have students play in pairs or groups of four (two teams of two).

25. Designate and share a storage area for the *Sunshine* materials. This encourages students to be self-sufficient in gathering the materials whenever there is time allotted to independently play the game.

MATH WORKSHOP AND SUMMARIZING THE EXPERIENCE

Teach this game at the beginning of the week to the whole class, then make it an integral part of your math workshop (for more on math workshop, see *Math Workshop* by Jennifer Lempp). Come together later in the week and hold a whole-class discussion. Ask questions that get at the scoring portion of the game like, "Were there any players that earned the additional ten points on the top portion? How about the bottom portion, did any players get two parallel and two perpendicular lines in three rolls or less?" Facilitate a "Give and Go" share (see the Teaching Tip).

ASSESSMENT

After students have had multiple opportunities to practice the game independently, use the *Sunshine* Assessment (REPRODUCIBLE 36) to further check their understanding.

TEACHING TIPS
Emphasizing Collaboration

For Part III, "Active Engagement," students should test the game out in teams of two with their partner, not playing against him or her. The goal is for students to work together in understanding *how* to play the game and the math that is involved. When students have the opportunity to play the game independently (Part IV), they then can play each other.

Managing Materials

You may choose to store sets of five dice in the cups; alternatively, stack the cups and keep each set of dice together in a separate container, small box, or sandwich bag.

Give and Go Sharing

Use a "Give and Go" sharing method for summarizing the lesson. Make sure each student has a completed score sheet from one of their games. Ask each student to pick out a row/category to highlight (alternatively, they can think of an overall strategy for approaching the game). Then students mingle, walking around the classroom and finding another student to pair up with. They each "give" their strategy for the game while showing their game sheet. When both students in a pair are done sharing, they "go" and find a new peer to do the same. This is an efficient, fun way to get many ideas shared. Typically three to five minutes is plenty of time for this type of sharing.

DIFFERENTIATING YOUR INSTRUCTION
Grouping Students

Based on your observations during the previous rounds of play with students, you may decide that certain students will benefit from playing in a team of two at "The Link" (Part IV) stage of learning, whereas others may be ready to play the game in pairs, one on one.

Volume 9

Recommended Grade 5

Time Instruction: 30–45 minutes
Independent Play: 15–20 minutes

TIME SAVER
Managing Materials
Precount the cubes into sets of 90 and store each set within individual containers or gallon-size baggies. This will help optimize instructional time as well as independent play.

Overview

The setup and playing of this game supports students in developing their understanding of volume. To begin, students, in pairs, create a "cube building" using 90 interlocking cubes. The building's dimensions are 3 by 3 by 10 for a volume of 90 cubic units. Students then take turns, choosing to remove one or two cubes from the top layer until the next, smaller cube building is formed. The last player to remove a cube or cubes to reveal the "new" top layer has the opportunity to identify the volume of the "new" building. If correct, the player earns a point. If the player incorrectly identifies the volume, the next player gets an opportunity to earn the point. Students continue, alternating turns and identifying the new volume of their cube building as each new top layer is revealed. The player who removes the cube or cubes revealing the original base layer and "Volume 9" earns two points. The player with the most points at the end of the game is the winner.

Materials

- interlocking cubes, 90 per pair of students
- paper, 1 sheet per pair of students
- pencil, 1 per pair of students
- *Volume 9* Game Directions (REPRODUCIBLE G-23A), 1 per pair of students

Related Game

Game 19: Mosaic

Key Questions

- What is the volume of your cube building at the start of the game? Explain how you know.
- What is the volume of your cube building after revealing a new top layer? Explain how you know.
- How is volume measured?
- How can you use repeated addition or multiplication in determining volume?

Teaching Directions

Part I: The Connection

Relate the game to students' ongoing work.

Show students a photo of a well-known sky-scraper or reference a building with multiple floors in their city (for example, a hotel). Task students with envisioning riding an elevator in the building. As they ride up the elevator, they pass different floors. Each floor takes up space. Tell students that the space that makes up each floor is called *volume*. Today they will construct a "building" out of interlocking cubes.

If this is students' first time using interlocking cubes, provide a minute or so for free play with the cubes. Even older students will have a desire to experiment with the interlocking cubes first.

Part II: The Teaching

Introduce and model the game to students.

1. Share with students that they will be learning how to play the game *Volume 9*. If students don't already have cubes, give each student 9 interlocking cubes. Task them, at their desks, with building a 3-by-3 square base.

2. Once students have each created a 3-by-3 square base, pair them up and have them snap their base to their partner's base. This forms a "building" that is 3 by 3 by 2 (a volume of 18 cubic units). (**Note:** It is important that the two bases connect and not just rest upon each other.)

 LEARNING TARGETS

Post the game's Learning Targets for students to see. This helps reinforce what students are responsible for learning as they play the game.

Grade 5:

- I can recognize volume as an attribute of solid figures.
- I know a solid figure, packed without gaps or overlaps, using n unit cubes is said to have a volume of n cubic units.
- I can determine volume by counting unit cubes.
- I can relate volume to the operations of multiplication and addition.

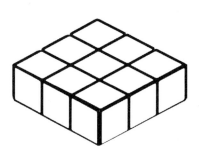

TEACHING TIP
Learning Targets

Step 3 is a good time in the lesson to post the Learning Targets and/or revisit them with students. Students will have just discussed volume as counting unit cubes and applying formulas $V = l \times w \times h$ and $V = b \times h$. It is important to share Learning Targets so students clearly know what is expected of them when playing games.

TEACHING TIPS
Selecting Student Volunteers

Be deliberate about who you select as the student volunteer to assist you in demonstrating the game. Select a student who is secure in their knowledge, because they will be put in a situation in which all of their peers are watching them.

Connecting the Learning

Often, students will not make the connection between the stated volume and the cubes. This is an opportunity to use your cube building to visually show the remaining 27 cubes and how this equates to volume. Write *27 units*³ where all students can see. Tell students that the little three that "floats" where an apostrophe mark would be represents volume. Volume is three-dimensional because it has length, width, and height.

3. Hold up your demonstration cube building of 3 by 3 by 2. Instruct students to discuss the volume of the cube building. Say, "With your partner, discuss two different ways to determine the volume."

4. Now have each pair of students partner up with another pair of students to form teams of four. Students then snap all their bases together so that their building is now 3 by 3 by 4 (a volume of 36 cubic units). While students are doing this, snap 18 more cubes to your demonstration cube building, so that it also has the same dimensions.

5. Next, share how to make the first move in the game *Volume 9*. Players take turns removing cubes from the top layer of their building (emphasize that it must be only from the top layer). On their turn they have the choice of removing one cube or two; the player who removes the last one or two cubes from the top layer then has the opportunity to earn a point if they can correctly identify the new volume of the cube building.

6. Ask for a student volunteer. Demonstrate Step 5 with your cube building while students look on. As the student volunteer and you take turns removing one or two cubes, task the remaining students with visualizing how many cubes will ultimately be in the top layer of the new building.

7. When the student volunteer or you remove the last cube(s) from the top layer, state the new volume out loud. This is a great opportunity to emphasize to students that volume is expressed in cubic units. Say, "Simply stating 'twenty-seven' would be incorrect. 'Twenty-seven cubic units' or 'twenty-seven units cubed' are the correct ways to express the new volume."

8. Share with students what happens if the player who removes the last one or two cubes of the top layer does not correctly state the volume.

In this case, the player whose turn it is next gets the opportunity to correctly express the volume. If they do so, they earn the point (essentially "stealing" it from the previous player). Finally, the player who removes the cube or cubes revealing the original base layer and "Volume 9" earns two points. This would be a good time to share the scoring of this game:

4 × 4 × 4 (1 point)

3 × 3 × 3 (1 point)

2 × 2 × 2 (1 point)

1 × 1 × 1 (2 points)

Part III: Active Engagement

Engage students to ensure they understand how to play the game.

9. Now give students an opportunity to explore an abbreviated version of the game in pairs. A typical game is played with 90 cubes—meaning the cube building that players start with is ten layers of 9 cubes. In the abbreviated version, have each pair of students start with 36 cubes.

10. As students are playing, circulate. Clarify misunderstandings and confirm correct play. Ask questions to check students' understanding (see "Key Questions," page 133). Have students play at least two games (this means they will deconstruct their cube building and then rebuild it using the exact same dimensions), so you have time to observe every pair or group.

Part IV: The Link

Students play the game independently.

11. Set students up for independent practice with the game. This time give each pair 90 cubes as well as paper and pencil for tracking points. As needed, also distribute copies of the *Volume 9* Game Directions (REPRODUCIBLE G-23A).

TEACHING TIPS
Pairing Students
Random pairings for this game work fine. You may also consider having students work in groups of four (two teams of two). The winning team then plays the winning team from another group, and the losing team plays the losing team. This gives students the opportunity to play with various peers, all of whom may have different strategies, varying math skills, and different ways of determining volume.

The Importance of Practice
Refrain from discussing game strategy during the Active Engagement part of the lesson. The purpose is to give students as much practice as possible first; they will then have the opportunity to come back later and discuss their experiences.

DIFFERENTIATING YOUR INSTRUCTION

Two Colors of Cubes

You might find it helpful to create the sets of 90 cubes so that they consist of two colors of cubes only (45 cubes of one color and 45 of another). Then, when students create their cube buildings, have them alternate colors, using one color of cubes per layer. This allows visual learners and/or struggling students to see the layers more easily.

125 Cubes

Introduce a variation of the game *Volume 9* using the *Volume 25* Game Directions **(REPRODUCIBLE G-23B)**. In this version students begin with 125 cubes and make a 5-by-5-by-5 cube building.

ASSESSMENT

After students have had multiple opportunities to practice the game independently, use the *Volume 9* Assessment **(REPRODUCIBLE 37)** to further check their understanding.

12. Ask students to visualize what their cube building will look like if the bottom layer is 3 by 3. What will the dimensions be? Have students show you with their hands about how tall or what the approximate height of a 3-by-3-by-10 cube building would be.

13. Designate and share a storage area for the cubes. This encourages students to be self-sufficient in gathering them whenever there is time allotted to independently play the game.

MATH WORKSHOP AND SUMMARIZING THE EXPERIENCE

Teach this game at the beginning of the week to the whole class, then make it an integral part of your math workshop (for more on math workshop, see *Math Workshop* by Jennifer Lempp). Note their individual skill level; come together later in the week and hold a discussion about how both skill and strategy played a role in the game. Ask students, "Was skill or strategy or both involved in this game? Explain."

Consider using think-pair-share when facilitating this discussion. Students first think quietly to themselves, formulating their thoughts. After some time has passed, students pair with other students to discuss their ideas. Lastly students share their thinking with the rest of the class (this last part is typically teacher-facilitated for efficiency). Think-pair-share is brain-compatible, engaging, and found in *Thinking Strategies for Student Achievement* by Denise D. Nessel and Joyce M. Graham, a book recommended by the National Urban Alliance.

Reproducibles

The following reproducibles are referenced throughout the text. These reproducibles are available in a downloadable, printable format. Visit www.mathsolutions.com/myonlineresources and register your product for access using the key code MGGM. See page ix for instructions.

Game Directions   203

In addition to the reproducibles, each game also has a condensed page(s) of directions written for students. These reproducibles are numbered starting with the letter G.

ANYTHING BUT NOTHING ASSESSMENT

Name _____ Date _____

Describe how each of the three hexagons below is partitioned.

1.

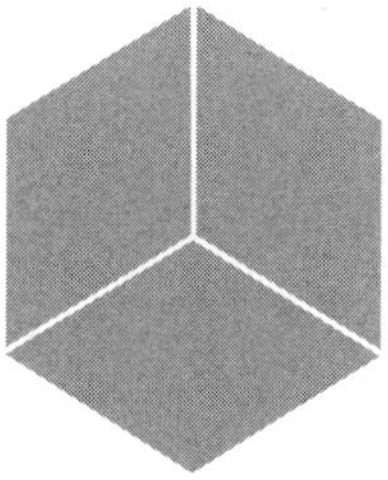

_____

_____

2.

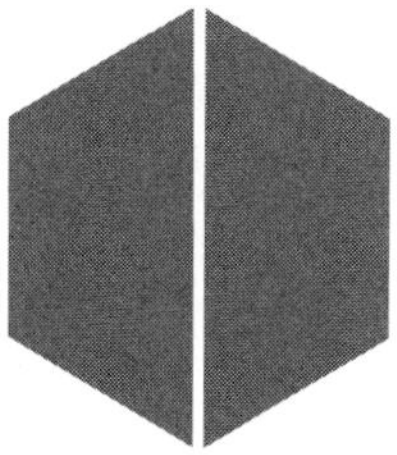

_____

_____

3.

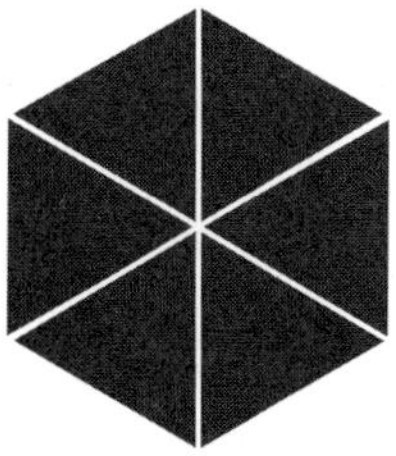

_____

_____

ANYTHING BUT NOTHING
ASSESSMENT, continued

Partition the rectangle below into fourths.

AREA STAYS THE SAME CARDS

Reproducible 2

One deck is a double-sided copy of each of the matching front and
back of this 10-page reproducible, totaling 30 cards.

Side: Front 1

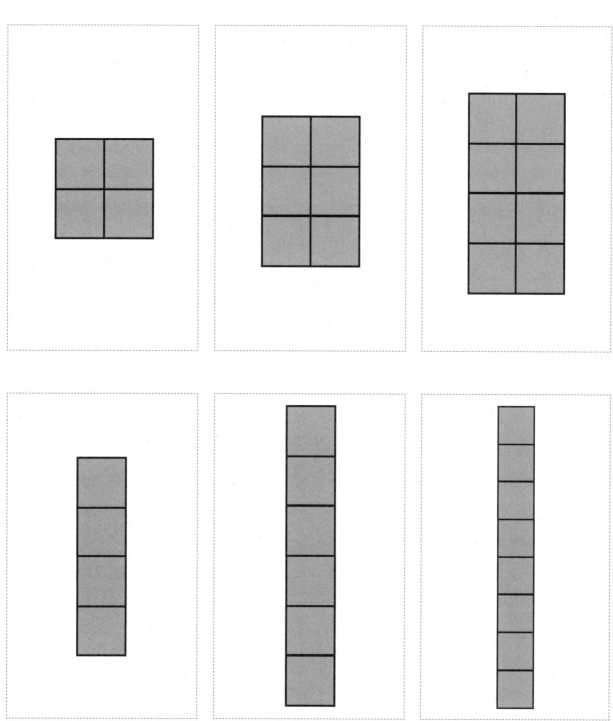

Side: Back 1

8   6   4

8   6   4

AREA STAYS THE SAME CARDS, continued

Side: Front 2

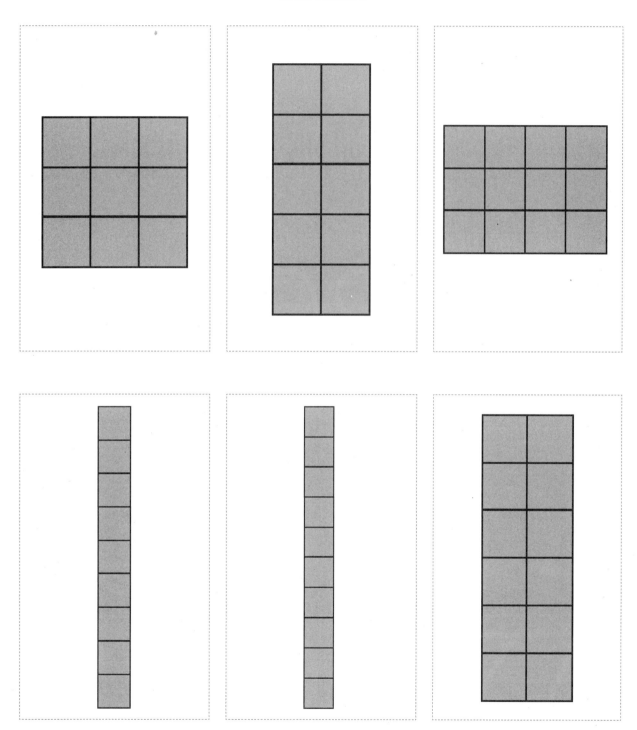

Side: Back 2

12   10   9

12   10   9

AREA STAYS THE SAME CARDS, continued

Side: Front 3

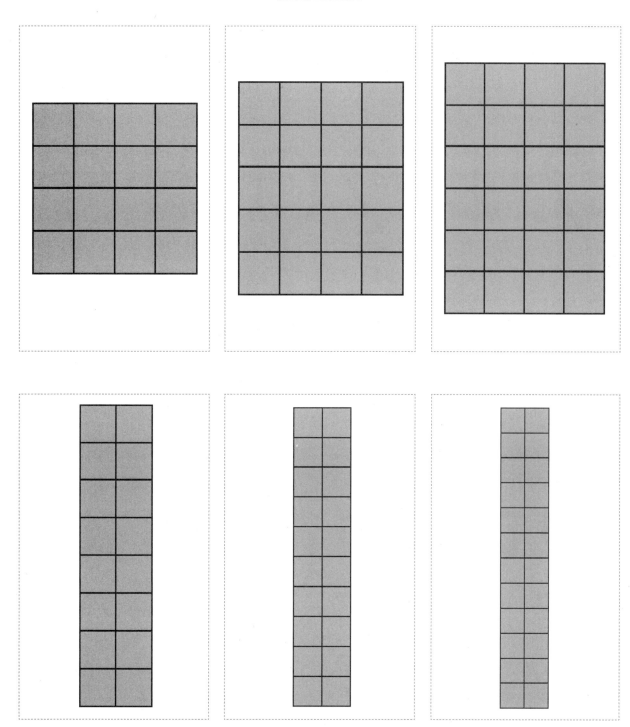

24 20 16

24 20 16

AREA STAYS THE SAME CARDS, continued

Side: Front 4

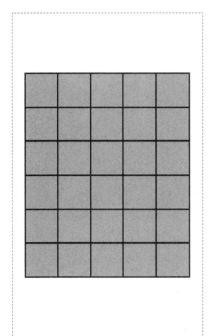

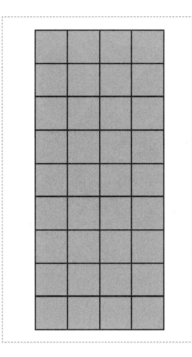

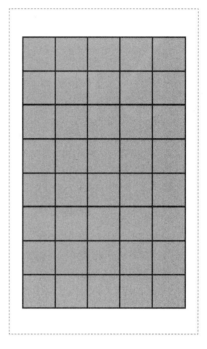

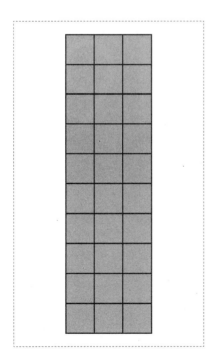

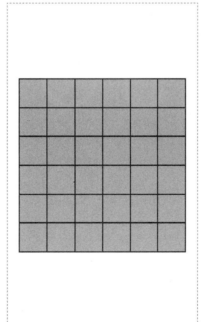

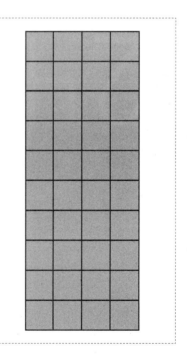

40   36   30

40   36   30

AREA STAYS THE SAME CARDS, continued

Side: Front 5

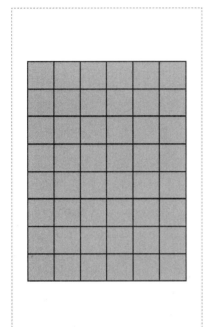

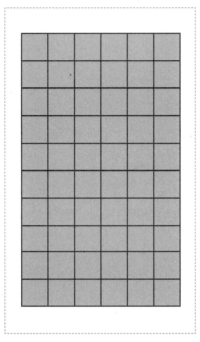

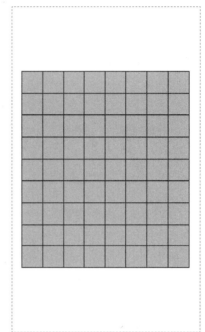

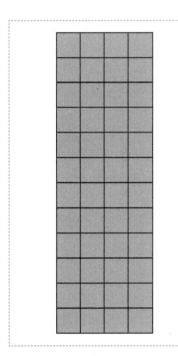

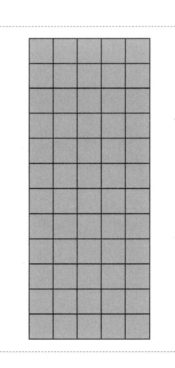

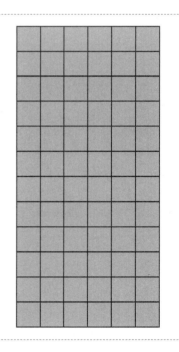

72 60 48

72 60 48

ATTRIBUTES ALIKE CARDS

One deck is four copies of this three-page reproducible, each copy in a different color (blue, green, red, yellow). This means a deck will have 18 cards of each of the four colors, or 72 cards total.

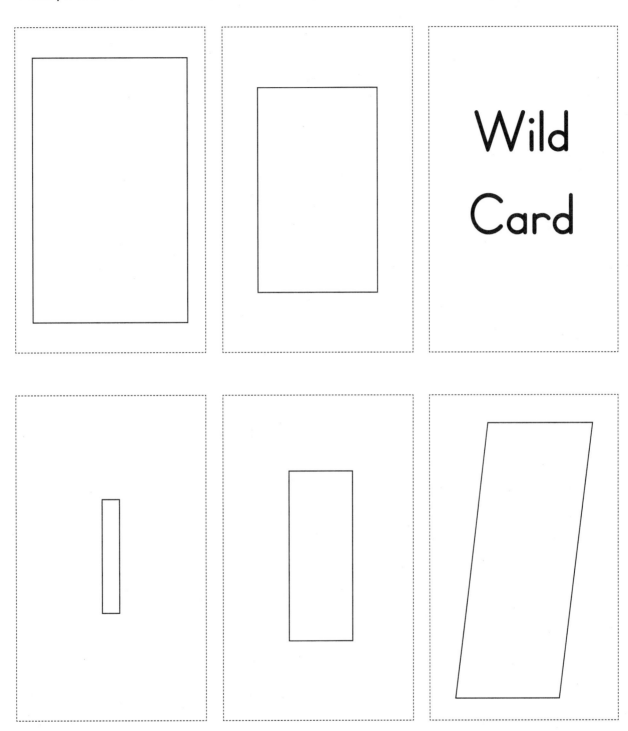

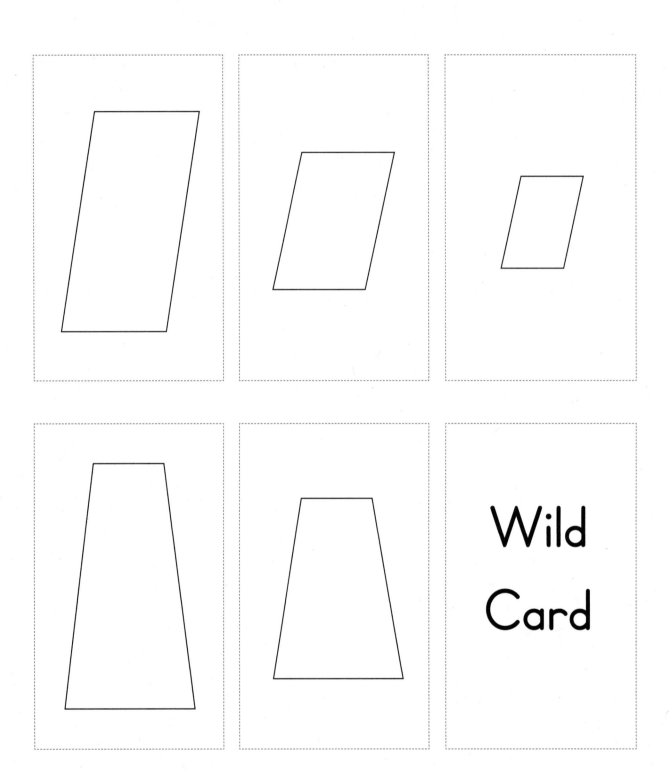

Wild Card

ATTRIBUTES ALIKE CARDS, continued

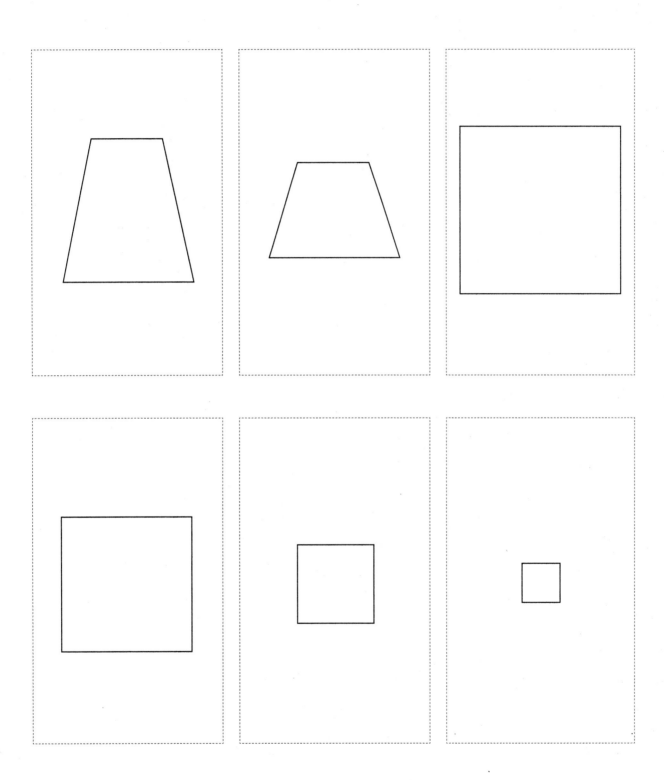

BOXED IN GAME BOARD

Copy the game board as needed to play the game (one game board for each game).

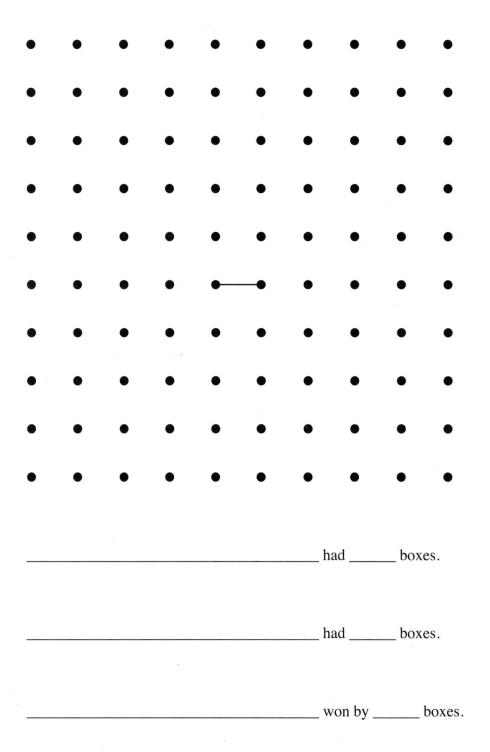

_____ had _____ boxes.

_____ had _____ boxes.

_____ won by _____ boxes.

BOXED IN SPINNER

Copy this spinner as needed to play the game, one spinner per pair of players.

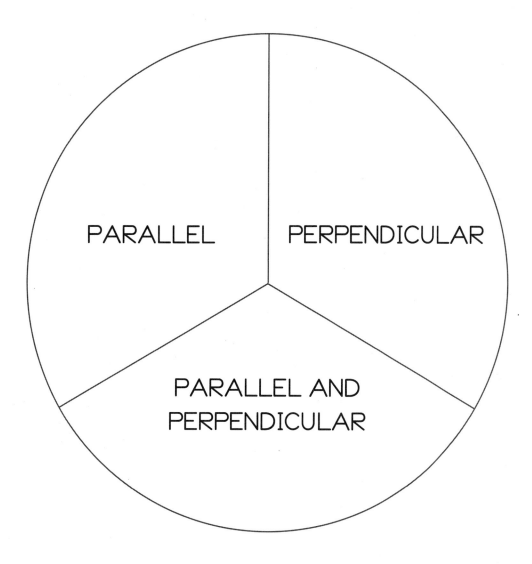

1. Pass out one large paper clip per pair of players.

2. Use the tip of a pencil to keep the paper clip on the spinner.

3. Spin the paper clip while holding the pencil or have a partner hold the pencil while you spin the paper clip.

BOXED IN MY ART

Name _____ Date _____

BOXED IN ASSESSMENT

Name _____ Date _____

Jin and Bojan are playing a game of *Boxed In*. This is what their game board looks like at one point:

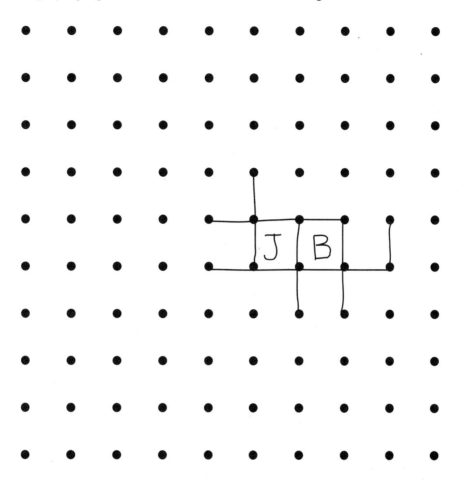

Identify two parallel lines on the game board. Place an X over them.

Identify two perpendicular lines on the game board. Circle them.

Now do the same for the following shapes. Does the shape have perpendicular lines? Parallel lines? Both? Circle the corresponding answer.

perpendicular	perpendicular	perpendicular	perpendicular
parallel	parallel	parallel	parallel
both	both	both	both

CIRCLE UP 360
PAPER PLATE TEMPLATE

Copy this template as needed to play the game (one copy per player). Alternatively, use actual paper plates and mark each with a starting ray like the one below.

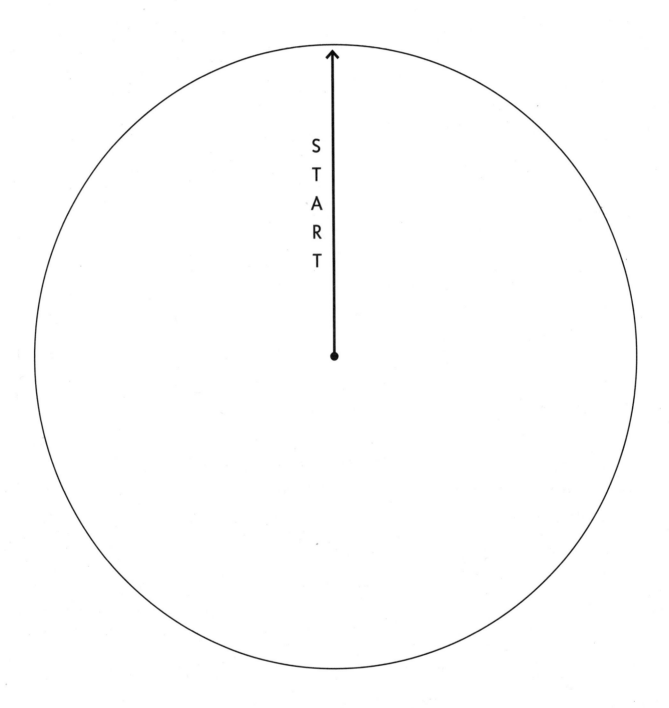

CLAIM THE DOTS GAME BOARD

Copy the game board as needed to play the game (one game board for each game).

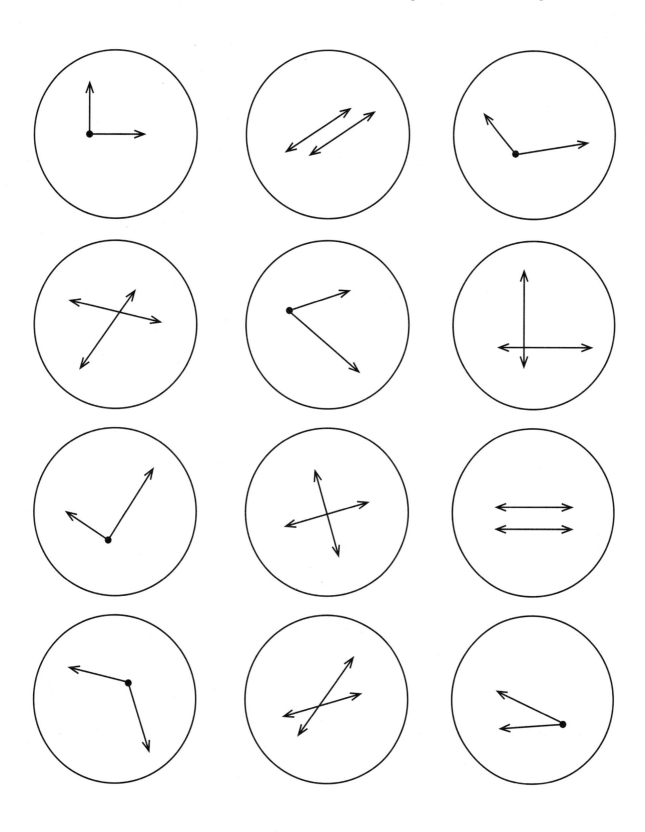

COMPARE (GEOMETRY VERSION)
POLYGON CARDS

One deck is two copies of each page of this five-page reproducible, totaling 54 cards.

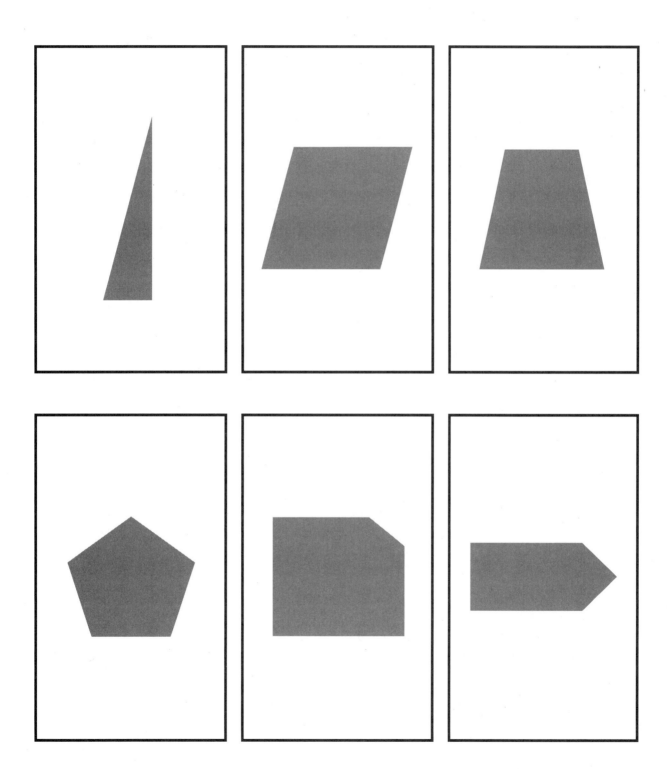

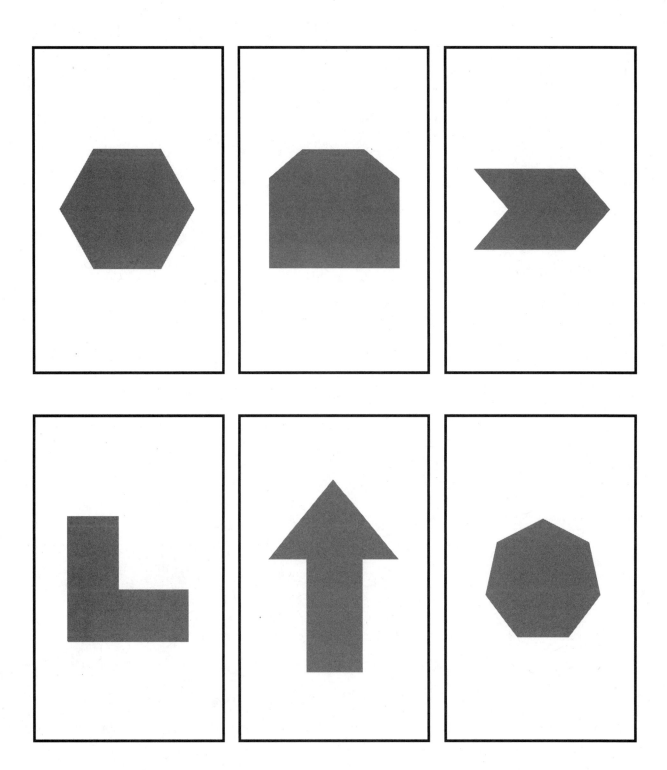

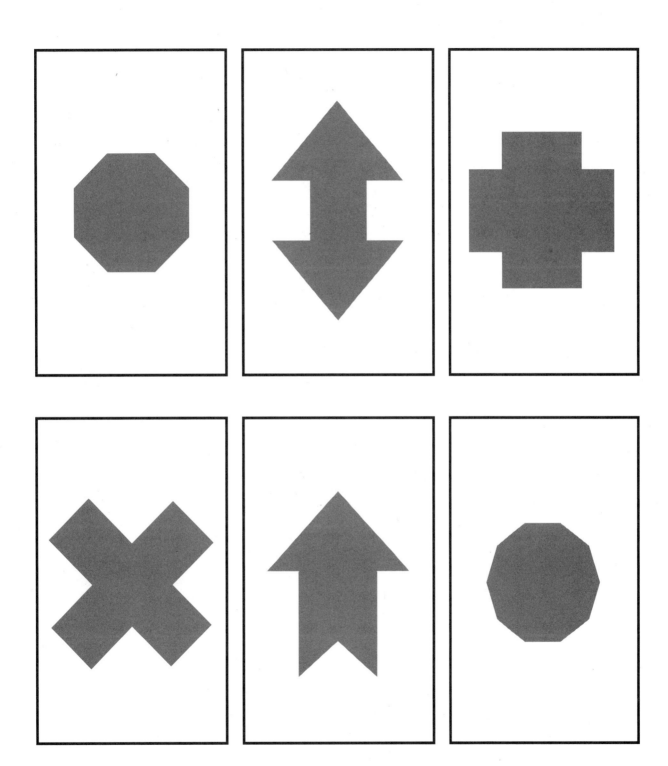

 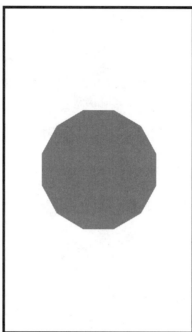 

COMPARE (MEASUREMENT VERSION) ASSESSMENT

Name _____ Date _____

Blake, Polina, and Rylie are playing the game of Compare. These are the cards they each drew in round one:

BLAKE	POLINA	RYLIE

1. Using interlocking cubes, build each of the three numbers into a cube stick.

2. Order the cube sticks from shortest to longest and place them on your paper in the space below.

3. Using a pencil, trace around each cube stick.

4. Label each cube stick tracing with the player's name and number of cubes in the stick.

5. Finally, complete these sentence frames:

   Blake's stick of cubes is _____ longer than Polina's.

   Polina's stick of cubes is _____ longer than Rylie's.

CONNECT FOUR GAME BOARD

Copy the game board as needed to play the game (one game board per game for each pair of players)

Player 1's Coordinates _____

Player 2's Coordinates _____

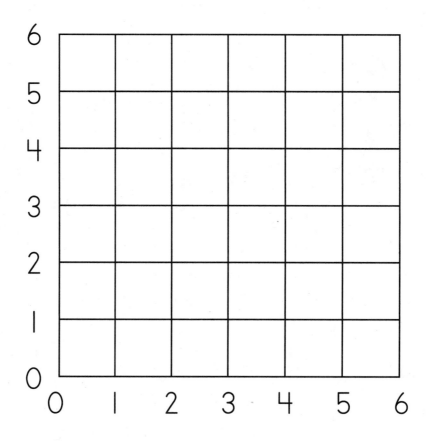

CONNECT FOUR ASSESSMENT

Name _____ Date _____

Below is a *Connect Four* game board. Player 1, Jonas, is playing with the black counters. Jonas is hoping to roll a 5, 3 so that he can have four in a row.

Is Jonas's thinking correct? Why or why not?

_____

_____

_____

_____

_____

_____

Player 2, Sasha, is playing with the grey counters. What coordinates would allow to Sasha to get four in a row? _____

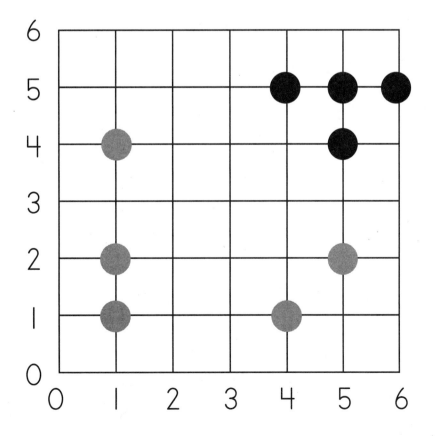

COORDINATES SECRECY
RECORDING CHART AND GAME BOARD 1

Copy this recording chart and game board as needed to play the game,
one copy per group of 2–4 players.

Coordinates	Number	Order

COORDINATES SECRECY
RECORDING CHART AND GAME BOARD 2

Copy this recording chart and game board as needed to play the game,
one copy per group of 2–4 players.

Coordinates	Number	Order	+/–

COORDINATES SECRECY
RECORDING CHART AND GAME BOARD 2,
continued

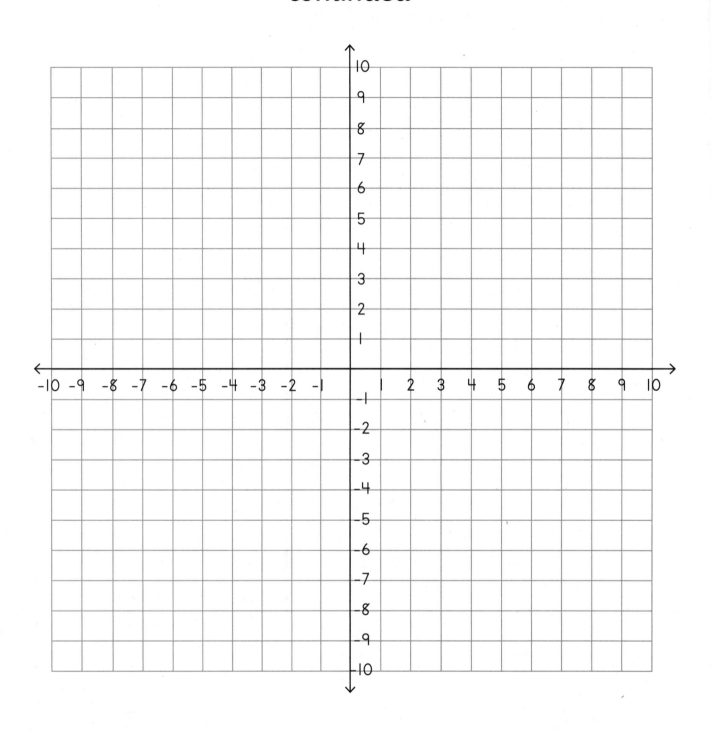

COORDINATE TIC-TAC-TOE
RECORDING CHART AND GAME BOARD 1

Copy this recording chart and game board as needed to play the game
(one copy per game for each pair of players).

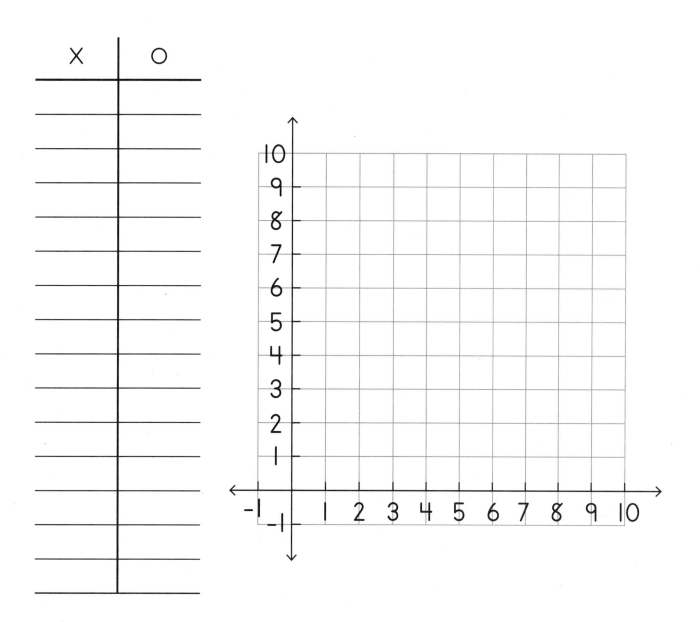

COORDINATE TIC-TAC-TOE
RECORDING CHART AND GAME BOARD 2

Copy this recording chart and game board as needed to play the game
(one copy per game for each pair of players).

X	O

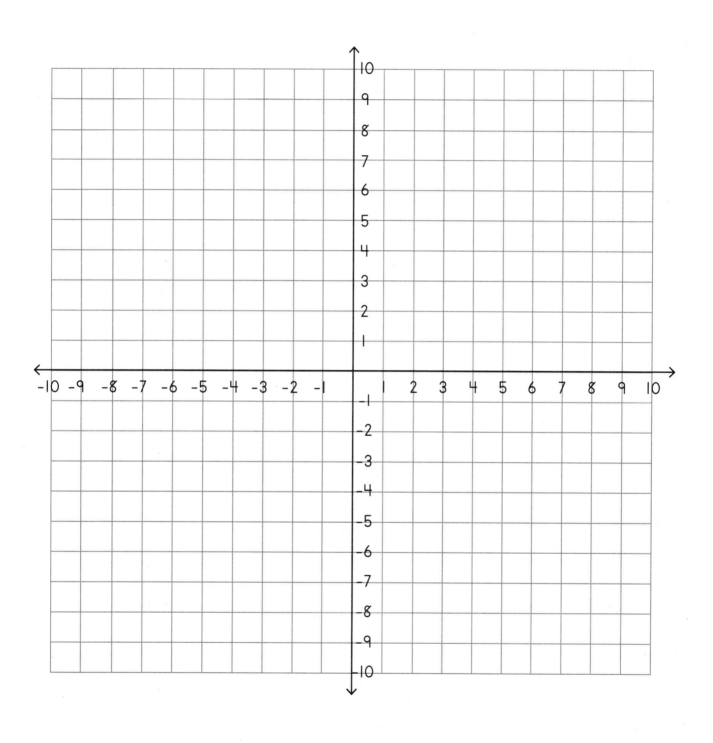

DESKTOP SHUFFLEBOARD
RECORDING SHEET 1

Name _____ Date _____

Measure each of the items below and record your findings in the Measurement column.

ITEM	MEASUREMENT
Dry Erase Marker	Inches: Centimeters:
Orange Pattern Block	Inches: Centimeters:
New (Unsharpened) Pencil	Inches: Centimeters:
Width of Paper	Inches: Centimeters:
Length of Paper	Inches: Centimeters:

DESKTOP SHUFFLEBOARD
RECORDING SHEET 2

Copy this sheet as needed to play the game (one chart per game).

	PLAYER 1 NAME:	PLAYER 2 NAME:
Unit of Measurement (circle one): centimeters or inches		
TURN 1		
TURN 2		
TURN 3		
TURN 4		
TURN 5		
TURN 6		
TURN 7		
TURN 8		
TURN 9		
TURN 10		

FOUR SQUARE GAME BOARD

Copy the game board as needed to play the game
(one game board per game for each group of players).

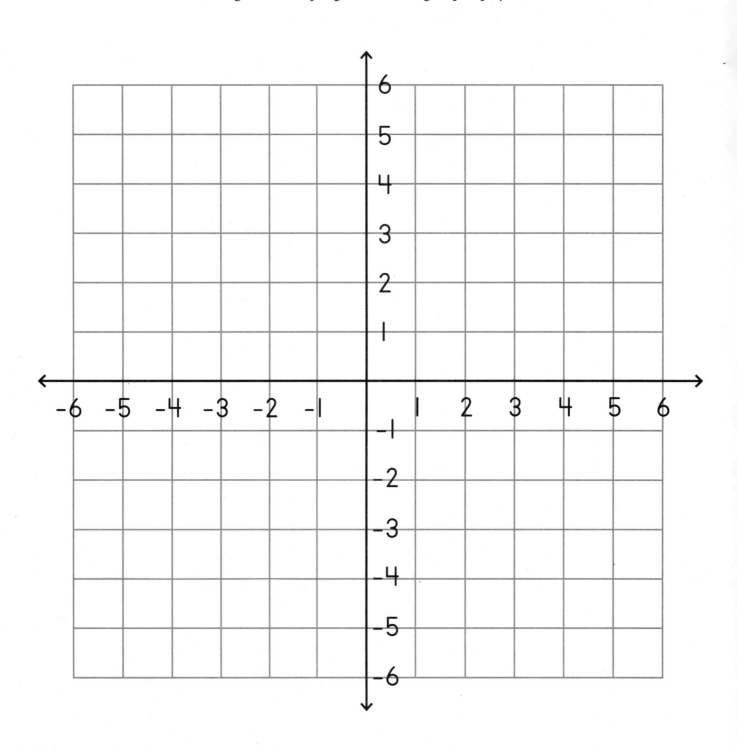

FOUR SQUARE ASSESSMENT

Graph the following points on the coordinate plane and label them accordingly.

COORDINATES	LABEL
3, 5	A
-3, 5	B
3, -5	C
-3, -5	D

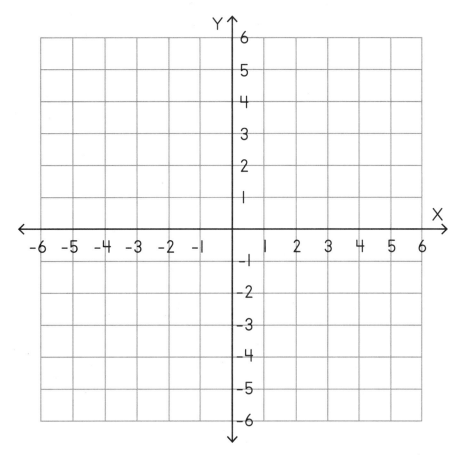

Write a reflection about how you determined the points plotted. Apply content vocabulary (*x*-axis and *x*-coordinate, *y*-axis and *y*-coordinate) in your explanation.

_____

_____

_____

_____

GEOMETRY GO FISH
CARDS, 2-D Shapes

One deck is one copy of this five-page reproducible, totaling 30 cards.

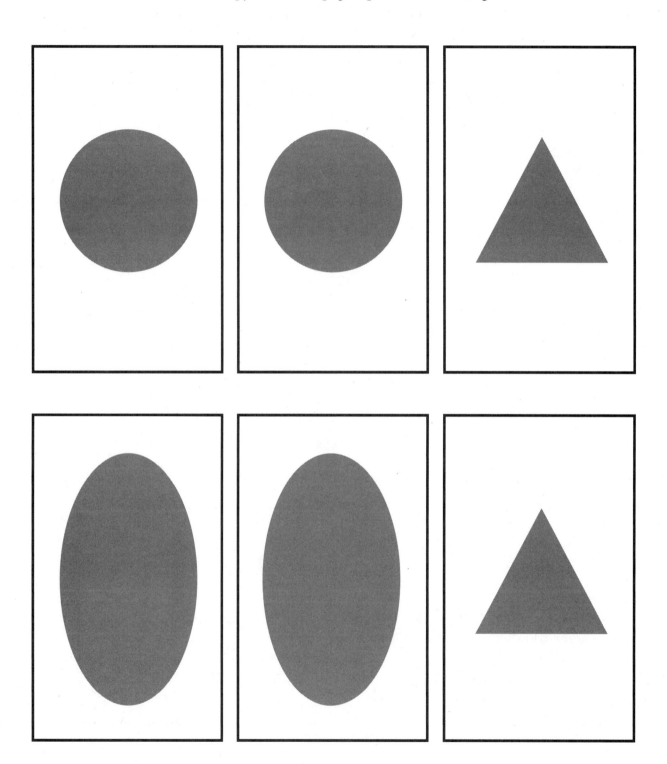

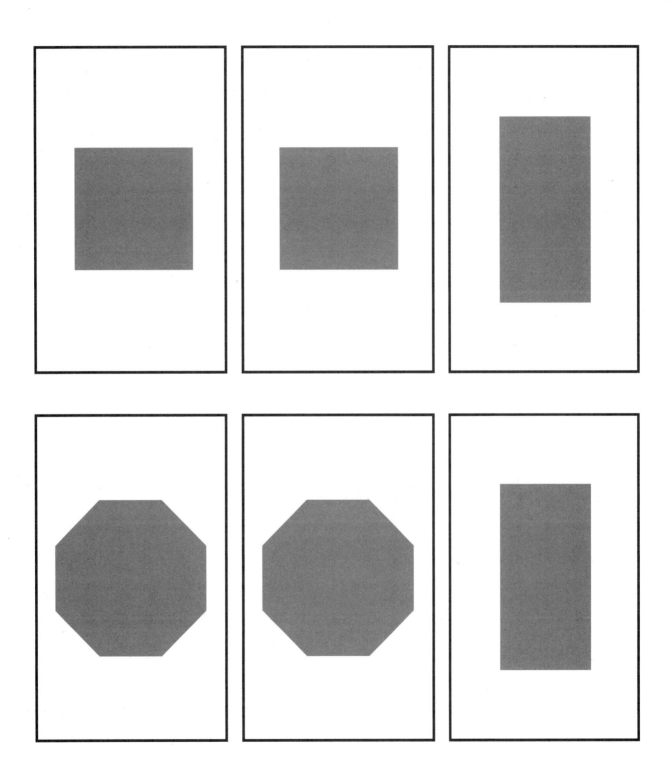

GEOMETRY GO FISH
CARDS, 2-D Shapes, continued

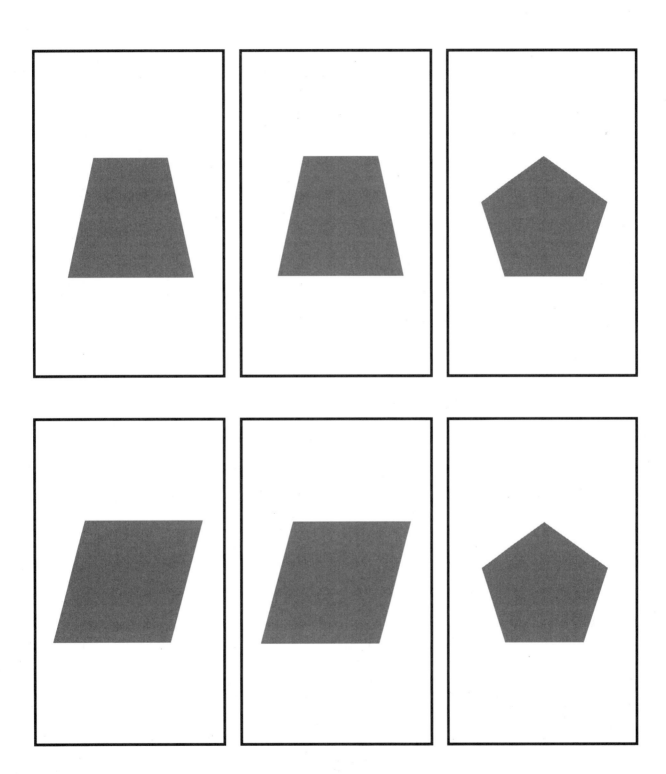

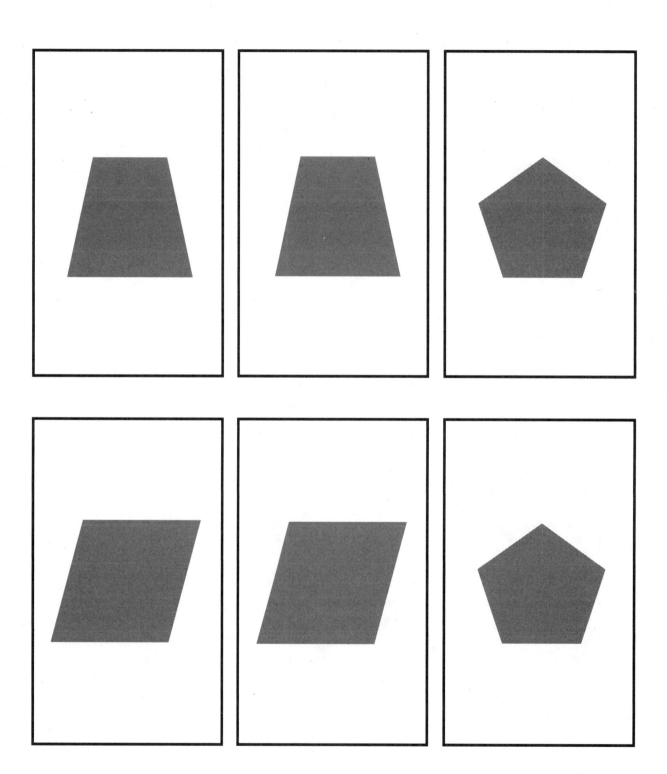

GEOMETRY GO FISH CARDS,
3-D Shapes

Add one copy of these cards to the deck created with
Reproducible 22 to have a deck featuring both 2-D and 3-D shapes.

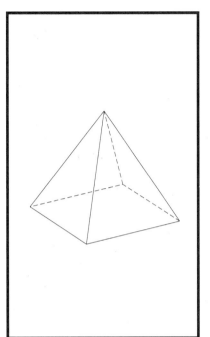
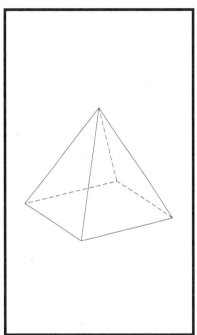

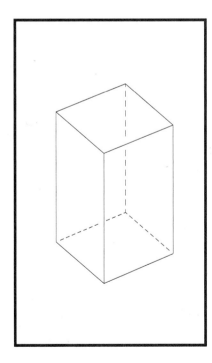
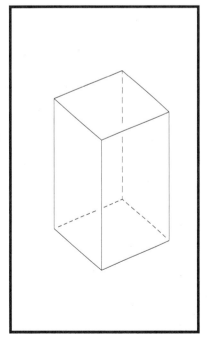

GEOMETRY GO FISH CARDS,
3-D Shapes, continued

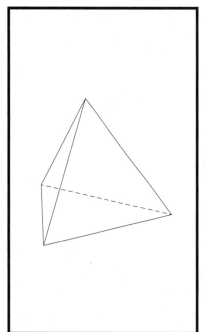

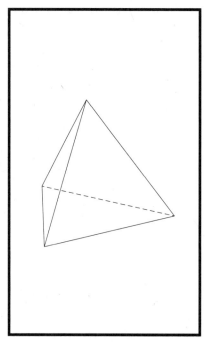

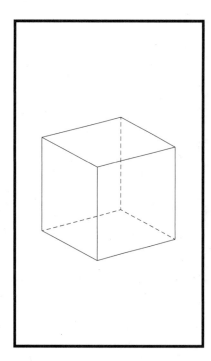

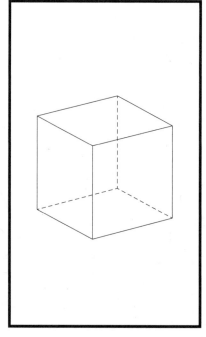

GO THE DISTANCE RECORDING SHEET   Reproducible 24
(CUSTOMARY VERSION)

Copy this recording sheet as needed to play the game, one
sheet for each player for one game (ten rounds).

Name _____ Date _____

Roll	Inches	Feet	Running Total
1			
2			
3			
4			
5			
6			
7			
8			
9			
10			

_____ is _____ away from 10 yards.

GO THE DISTANCE RECORDING SHEET (METRIC VERSION)

Reproducible 25

Copy this recording sheet as needed to play the game, one
sheet for each player for one game (ten rounds).

Name _____ Date _____

Roll	Millimeters	Centimeters	Running Total
1			
2			
3			
4			
5			
6			
7			
8			
9			
10			

_____ is _____ away from 1 meter.

HAVE TO HALVE ASSESSMENT

Name _____ Date _____

Suejin was playing *Have to Halve*. Below is what her geoboard looked like after several rounds of play.

1. Label each part in relationship to the whole. Use words like *half*, *fourth*, or *eighth* or use numbers like $\frac{1}{2}$, $\frac{1}{4}$, or $\frac{1}{8}$.

2. Suejin rolls an even number on her next roll and gets to add a band to partition the largest section. Shade the two parts where Suejin might make her move.

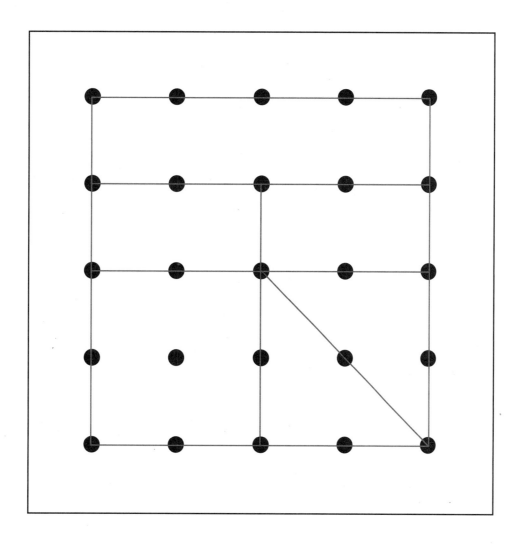

LINE PLOT TIC-TAC-TOE
GAME BOARD

Copy the game board as needed to play the game
(one game board per game for each pair of players).

MARCH TO THE METER
RECORDING SHEET

Use this recording sheet as another way to track your moves on the meter stick. Each time you roll, in addition to moving your game marker along the actual meter stick, place a mark on the meter stick below. Use a colored pencil or crayon that is the same color as your game marker.

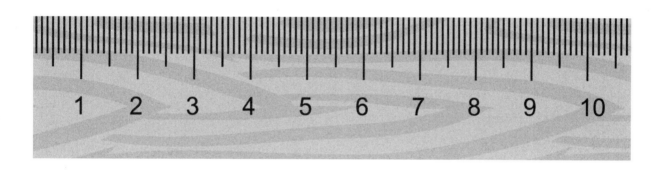

Player 1: _____   _____
                          Name   Color of Game Marker

Player 2: _____   _____
                          Name   Color of Game Marker

Player _____ won by _____ centimeters (cm).

The player who lost ended on _____ cm. Three real-world items that are approximately the same number of centimeters are:

1._____   2._____   3._____

MOSAIC ASSESSMENT

Name ______________________________ Date ______________

Show two ways you can determine the area of each figure below. Use the space next to each figure to show your work.

FIGURE A

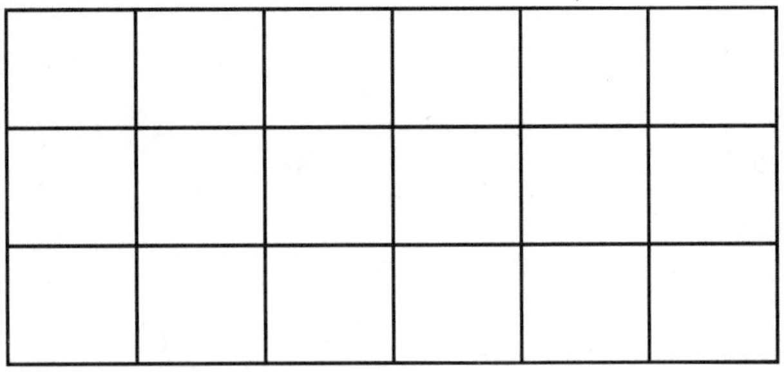

WORK SPACE

FIGURE B

WORK SPACE

FIGURE C

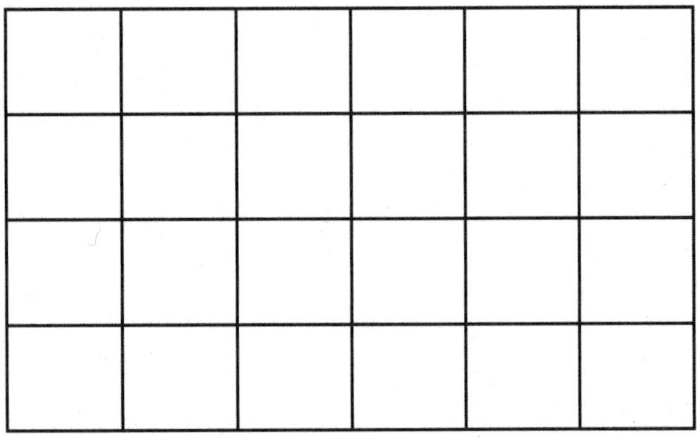

WORK SPACE

POSITIONS
SHAPE CARDS

One deck is 49 cards: two copies each of the first four pages of this
reproducible (totaling 48 shape cards) and one copy of the star card.

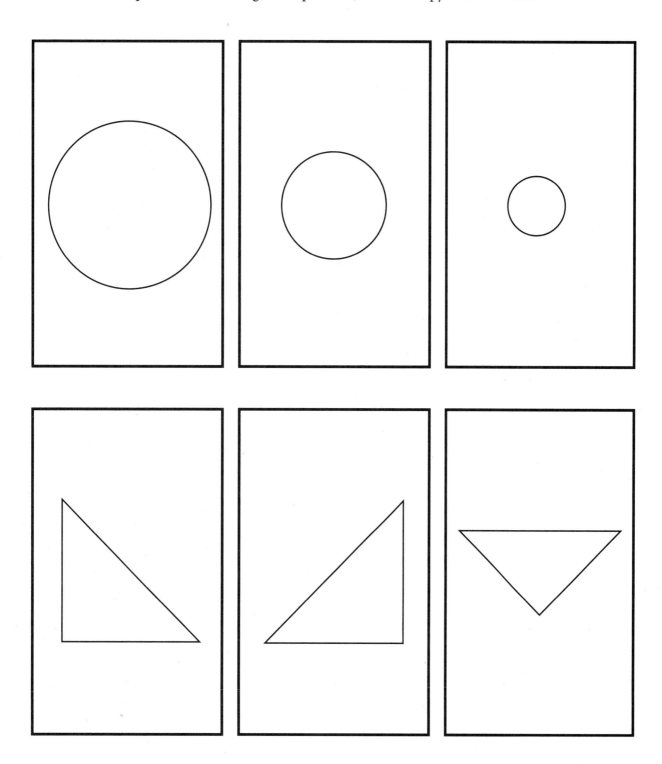

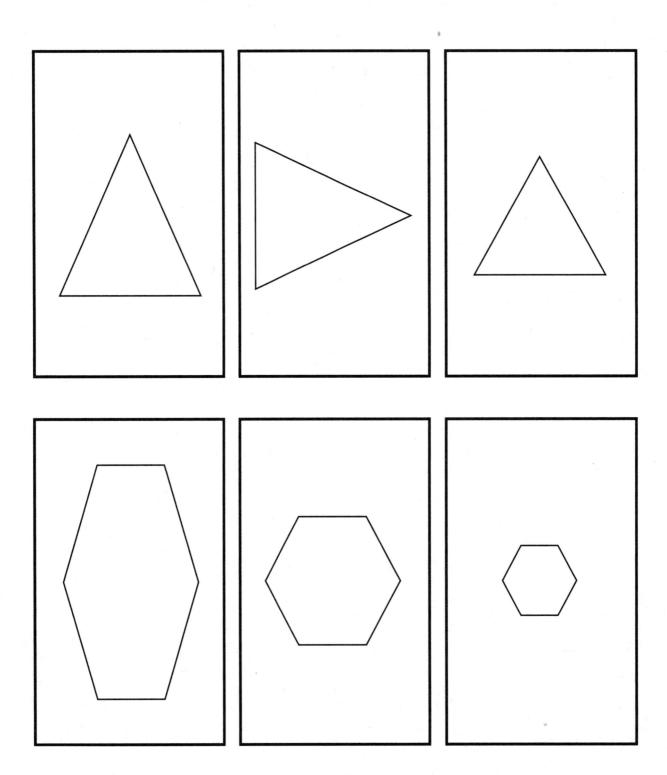

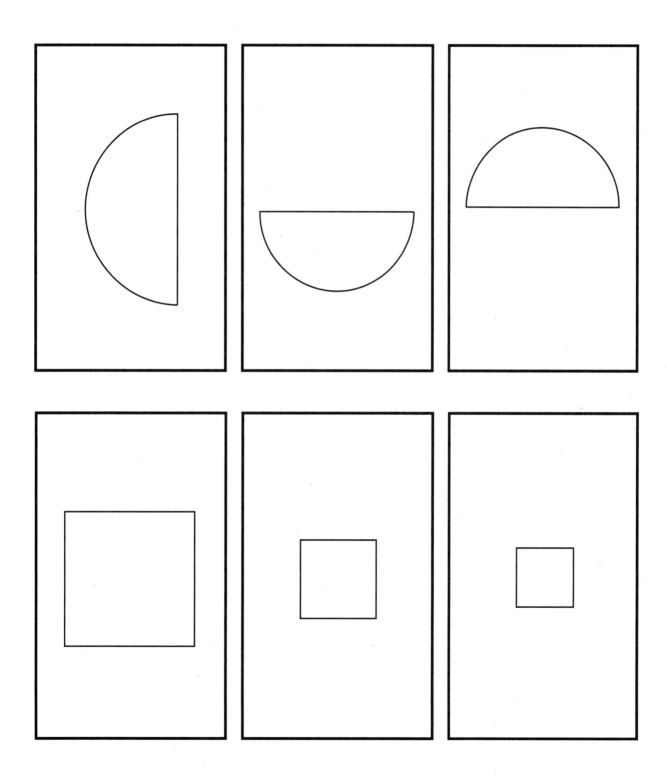

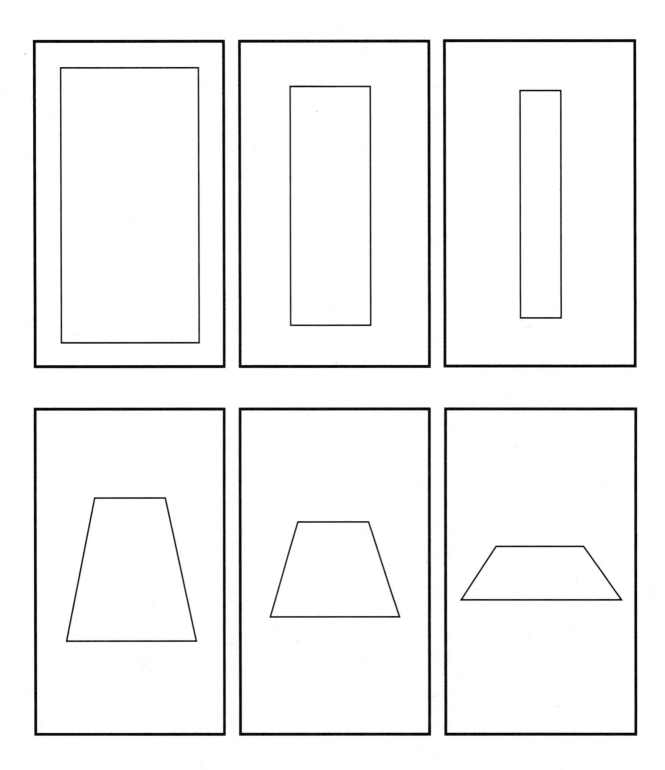

Reproducible 30

Make one copy of the star card for each deck.

POSITIONS SPINNER

Copy this spinner as needed to play the game, one spinner per group of players.

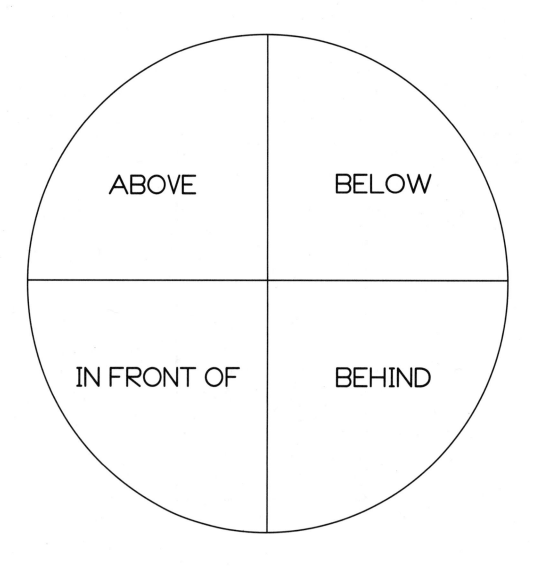

1. Pass out one large paper clip per group of players.

2. Use the tip of a pencil to keep the paper clip on the spinner.

3. Spin the paper clip while holding the pencil or have another player hold the pencil while you spin the paper clip.

POSITIONS ASSESSMENT

Name _____ Date _____

Below is a game set up for *Positions*. Each shape is placed around the star in the middle. Do the following:

- Color the shape in the position "above" the star red.

- Color the shape in the position "in front of" the star blue.

- Color the shape in the position "behind" the star green.

- Color the shape in the position "below" the star orange.

BONUS: Write the name of the shape by each card.

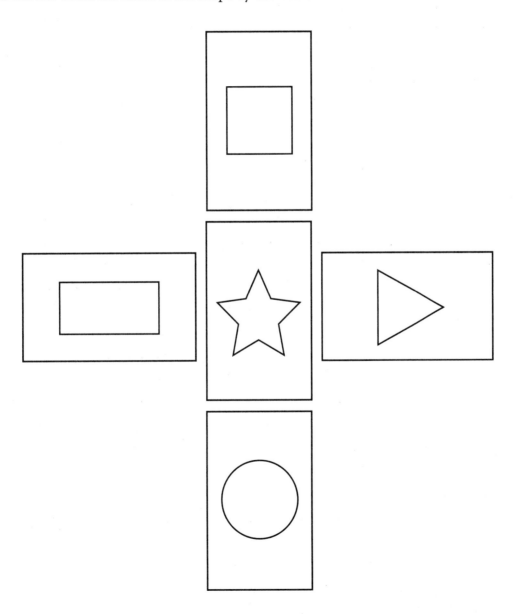

ROLL FIVES TO 60 GAME BOARD

Copy the game board as needed to play the game (one game board for each player).

ROLL FIVES TO 60
EXTENSION GAME BOARD

Copy the game board as needed to play the game (one game board for each player).

SUNSHINE SCORE SHEET

Make copies of these score sheets, cut the paper in half along the dashed
line to form two score sheets, and hand them out, one per player.

	1	2	3	4	5	total
point						
line						
line segment						
ray						
parallel						
perpendicular						
Total of the top portion:						
*If total for top portion is over 18, add 10 points.						
3 of a kind	Add 10 points.					
4 of a kind	Add 15 points.					
2 parallel & 2 perpendicular	Add 20 points.					
5 rays "SUNSHINE"	Add 25 points.					
Total of the bottom portion:						

Winner of the top: _____

Winner of the bottom: _____

Overall winner: _____

	1	2	3	4	5	total
point						
line						
line segment						
ray						
parallel						
perpendicular						
Total of the top portion:						
*If total for top portion is over 18, add 10 points.						
3 of a kind	Add 10 points.					
4 of a kind	Add 15 points.					
2 parallel & 2 perpendicular	Add 20 points.					
5 rays "SUNSHINE"	Add 25 points.					
Total of the bottom portion:						

Winner of the top: _____

Winner of the bottom: _____

Overall winner: _____

SUNSHINE ASSESSMENT

Name _____ Date _____

Draw the corresponding geometric symbol.

endpoint	line	line segment
ray	parallel lines	perpendicular lines

Identify the parallel lines in the following shapes; mark them in color.

Identify the perpendicular lines in the following shapes by marking the 90-degree angle created. Some shapes will have both parallel and perpendicular lines.

VOLUME 9 ASSESSMENT

Name _____ Date _____

Shirin and Jackson were playing *Volume 9*. Below are pictures of what the cube building looked like at one point in the game. Shirin says the volume is 27 cubic units. Jackson insists the volume is 26 cubic units.

Who is correct, Shirin or Jackson? Explain your reasoning.

_____

_____

_____

What is another way you could determine volume that is different from what you described above?

_____

_____

_____

Game 1: Anything but Nothing! (Partitioning Shapes)

Objective

During this game, players fully partition three hexagon pattern blocks—one into halves, another into thirds, and the last into sixths. Each player, in turn, rolls a fraction die to determine what pattern block to use to cover a hexagon. The first player to fully partition all three hexagons is the winner.

Materials

- pattern blocks, 1 set per player: 3 yellow hexagons, 2 red trapezoids, 3 blue rhombuses, 6 green triangles
- Anything but Nothing! fraction die (a die with six faces labeled: $\frac{1}{2}, \frac{1}{3}, \frac{1}{3}, \frac{1}{6}, \frac{1}{6}$ and the last face is blank)

Players

2–4

Directions

1. Each player places three hexagons from their pattern blocks set in front of them. They then each place their remaining pattern blocks in a pile near them.

2. Decide who is Player 1. Player 1 rolls the die. Two scenarios happen:

    - If the face with nothing is rolled (the blank face), the player's turn is over—nothing happens.

    - If any other face is rolled, the player selects the pattern block from her pile that represents the fractional part of the hexagon and aligns it on top of one of the three hexagons, partitioning off $\frac{1}{2}, \frac{1}{3},$ or $\frac{1}{6}$.

3. Player 1 may either end their turn or roll again. Three scenarios may happen if they choose to roll again:

    - If the face with nothing is rolled, all pattern blocks previously played during the entire game, not just the round, are removed from the player's hexagons and returned to the pile.

    - If the player rolls a fraction that cannot be played (i.e., $\frac{1}{2}$ is rolled but the hexagon being partitioned into halves is already fully covered) then the player's turn is over.

    - If any other face is rolled, the player selects the pattern block from her pile that represents the fractional part of the hexagon and aligns it on top of one of the three hexagons, partitioning off $\frac{1}{2}, \frac{1}{3},$ or $\frac{1}{6}$.

4. Play alternates.

5. The first player to fully partition all three hexagons—one into halves, one into thirds, and the last into sixths—is the winner.

Game 2:
Area Stays the Same

Objective

For this game, players place a set of *Area Stays the Same* cards, array side up, in the middle of the playing space. The cards are scattered about much like you would see them in a game of *Go Fish*. Players take turns selecting two cards that they believe show arrays with the same area. If correct, the player keeps the cards. If incorrect, the player returns the cards to the playing space. Once all the cards have been matched, the player with the most cards wins.

Materials

- *Area Stays the Same* Cards
  (REPRODUCIBLE 2, front and back), 1 deck

Players

2

A Deck of Cards
For the purpose of this game, a deck is 30 cards (1 copy of Reproducible 2, front and back).

Directions

1. Decide who is Player 1 and who is Player 2. Players place all of the cards in the middle of the playing space, the array side facing up.

2. Player 1 draws two cards from the middle that they believe show arrays with the same area.

3. Player 1 states the area of each array and then flips the card over to check to see if theirs is correct.

4. If theirs is correct, the player keeps the pair of cards. If theirs is incorrect, they return both cards to the middle of the playing space, with array side up.

5. Play alternates.

6. Once all the cards have been matched, the player with the most cards wins.

Game 3: Attributes Alike

Objective

This game is played similarly to *Uno*. Players take turns playing a card that has two attributes alike and one differing from the faceup card. If a player cannot play a card, they must draw one card from the top of the draw pile. Play continues until one player has played all their cards. Sometimes this requires the discard pile to be shuffled and restacked as the draw pile so play can continue.

Materials

- *Attribute Alike* Cards (REPRODUCIBLE 3), 1 deck

A Deck of Cards

For the purpose of this game, a deck of cards is four copies of the two-page reproducible, each copy in a different color (i.e., blue, green, red, yellow). This means a deck will have 18 cards of each of the four colors, or 72 cards total.

Players

2–4

Directions

1. Players shuffle the cards. Each player chooses seven or a dealer may be selected to deal seven cards to each player.

2. The remaining cards go facedown in a stack in the middle of the playing space; this is the draw pile. Flip the top card faceup and place it next to the draw pile; this is the start of the discard pile.

3. Players take turns playing cards with two attributes alike and one differing from the faceup card. When they have a "match," they place their card faceup on top of th existing one.

4. If a player is unable to make a play (doesn't have a "match"), he or she must draw a card from the draw pile. The player may play the card drawn if it works. If not, play moves on to the next player.

5. The first player to use all of the cards in his or her hand is the winner. Sometimes this requires the discard pile to be shuffled and restacked as the draw pile so play can continue.

Attributes

The attributes used in this game are color, shape, and size.

Game 4: Boxed In
(A Game of Parallel and Perpendicular Moves)

Objective

The game is similar to *Dots and Boxes*; however, players, in pairs, use a spinner to determine their next move. A spin determines one of three possible moves: parallel, perpendicular, or parallel and perpendicular. Players draw their line segment accordingly, connecting two dots on the game board. If a player closes a "box" (square) on their play, they claim the box by writing their initials in it. The goal is to create and claim the most boxes on the game board.

Materials

- *Boxed In* Game Board (REPRODUCIBLE 4)
- *Boxed In* Spinner (REPRODUCIBLE 5)
- paper clip
- pencil

Players

2

Directions

1. Decide who is Player 1 and who is Player 2.

2. Player 1 spins the spinner to determine one of three possible moves: parallel, perpendicular, or parallel and perpendicular. Player 1 draws a line segment accordingly, connecting two dots on the game board. Player 1's "move" must relate to the line segment predrawn in the middle of the game board. Player 2 confirms that Player 1's move (line segment) is correct.

3. Player 2 spins the spinner to determine one of three possible moves: parallel, perpendicular, or parallel and perpendicular. Player 2 draws a line segment accordingly, connecting two dots on the game board. Player 2's "move" must relate to the line segment that Player 1 previously drew. For example, if the spinner lands on "parallel," Player 2 draws a line segment that is parallel to Player 1's last line segment. If the spinner lands on the option marked "parallel and perpendicular," Player 2 gets to draw two line segments accordingly. Player 1 confirms that Player 2's move (line segment) is correct.

4. Play alternates, each player spinning the spinner and adding a line segment or segments to the game board, in relation to the previous line segment drawn. If a player makes a wrong move, the player erases the line and loses that turn.

5. When a player closes a box, they write their initials in the box.

6. A player loses a turn if their spin lands on an option that can no longer be done on the game board. Play ends when both players have spun three consecutive times and cannot make a move, or when players have claimed all of the boxes.

7. Players count their boxes. The player with the most boxes is the winner.

Game 5: Circle Up 360
(A Measurement Game Using Protractors)

Objective

In this game each player has her own game board—a paper plate. Players take turns drawing and labeling angles on their plates. After players have drawn six angles on each of their plates, they measure the remaining angle on each of their plates. The goal is to be the player with the smallest remaining angle on their plate.

Materials

- protractors, 2
- paper plates or *Circle Up 360* Paper Plate Template (REPRODUCIBLE 8), 2
- dice (labeled *1–6*), 2

Players

2

Directions

1. Decide who is Player 1 and who is Player 2.

2. Player 1 rolls both dice and creates a two-digit number from the numbers rolled. For example, if a 1 and a 5 are rolled, the two-digit number could be 15 or 51. This number is the measurement of the angle that Player 1 then needs to draw.

3. Using a protractor and the premarked starting ray on her paper plate, Player 1 draws the corresponding angle, working clockwise around the plate.

4. Player 2 checks Player 1's accuracy using a protractor. If Player 2 agrees that the measurement is right, Player 1 labels the angle accordingly.

5. Player 2 repeats Steps 1–2, rolling both dice and creating a two-digit number from the numbers rolled, then drawing the corresponding angle on his paper plate (working clockwise).

6. Player 1 checks Player 2's accuracy using a protractor. If Player 1 agrees the measurement is correct, Player 2 labels the angle accordingly.

7. Play alternates. Each player takes 6 turns total (working clockwise on their paper plates). The previous ray drawn is always the new starting ray (becoming part of the next angle).

8. After six rounds of play, players measure the remaining angle on each of their plates. The player with the smallest remaining angle is the winner.

Game 6: Claim the Dots
(Classifying Angles and Lines)

Objective

In this game, players roll a die and use the game's legend to translate the number to an angle or lines. They then place a transparent chip on the matching angle or lines on the game board. Once a chip has been placed, it can be secured with another of the same player's chips should they again roll the same angle or lines. If a player's chip is not secured with a second chip, their opponent can knock their chip off the game board should they roll the same angle or lines. Ultimately, the player with the most dots "claimed" wins the game.

Materials

- *Claim the Dots* Game Board (REPRODUCIBLE 9)
- dice (labeled *1–6*)
- transparent chips, 2 sets of 24, each set a different color

Players

2

Directions

1. Decide who is Player 1 and who is Player 2. Each player selects a set of chips, ensuring that it is a different-color set than their partner's.

2. Player 1 rolls the die. Using the game's legend, Player 1 places one of her chips on the matching angle or lines on the game board. For example, if a 5 is rolled, per the legend, Player 1 finds and covers a dot containing perpendicular lines on the game board.

3. Player 2 confirms that Player 1's move is accurate. If not, Player 1 removes her chip from the game board and her turn is over.

4. Player 2 then rolls the die and using the legend, places one of his chips on the matching angle or lines on the game board. Player 1 confirms that Player 2's move is accurate. If not, Player 2 removes his chip from the game board and his turn is over.

5. If Player 2 rolls a number that Player 1 already rolled, Player 2 has the opportunity to knock Player 1's chip off the board and place his chip on the dot instead.

6. Play alternates. If a player rolls a number he previously rolled, and his chip is still on the matching angle or lines, he can place a second chip over his first chip. When a chip has a second same-color chip on top of it, the chips can no longer be knocked off the board and the dot is "claimed" by that player.

7. The game board has two of each type of angle or lines. If a player rolls a number for an angle or lines that is already entirely claimed on the board, the player loses that turn.

8. Play ends when all dots are claimed or both players have rolled three consecutive times and cannot make a move. Each player then counts the number of dots they claimed (those dots that have two of their colored chips). The player with the most claimed dots wins.

Claim the Dots Legend

 Acute Angle   Intersecting Lines
(Intersecting but not Perpendicular)

Right Angle   Perpendicular Lines

Obtuse Angle   Parallel Lines

Game 7: Compare
(Geometry Version)

Objective

This game uses a special deck of polygon cards. Players shuffle, deal, and stack the cards in front of them. Each player draws the top card from their stack and places it faceup in the playing area. Whose card features the polygon with the most sides? That player "earns" both cards. When all cards have been played, players count their cards; the player with the most cards is the winner.

Materials

- *Compare (Geometry Version)* Polygon Cards (REPRODUCIBLE 10), 1 deck

Players

2

Directions

1. Decide who is Player 1 and who is Player 2. Shuffle the deck and deal, creating two equal stacks of cards. Each player places their stack of cards in front of them, facedown.

2. Each player draws the top card from their stack and places it faceup in the playing area.

3. Players compare the polygons on their cards—how many sides does each polygon have? The player whose card features the polygon with the most sides takes both cards—that player has "earned" two cards.

4. If the polygon on both cards has the same number of sides, the cards remain where they are and players draw the next top card from their stacks, this time placing the card faceup on top of the previous card. The player who has the card featuring the polygon with the most sides now sets aside all the drawn cards, including the two from the previous play (so the player earns four cards).

5. Once all the cards in both stacks have been played, players count the cards they've earned. The player with the most cards wins.

6. Total the two numbers; the two numbers should always add up to 54 because there are 54 cards in each deck.

A Deck of Cards

For the purpose of this game, a deck of cards is two copies of each page of the five-page reproducible. This means a deck will have 54 cards.

Game 8: Compare
(Measurement Version)

Objective

Players start the game by dealing a customized deck of numeral cards (1–10) or playing cards (Ace–10). Each player turns over the top card and uses interlocking cubes to build a stick of cubes corresponding to the number on their card. Next, players order and compare the lengths of their cube sticks. Each player earns points based on the difference in the number of cubes between their stick and the next shortest stick. Ultimately, the player who earns the most points (cubes) wins.

Materials

- numeral cards (1–10) or playing cards (Ace–10), 1 deck
- interlocking cubes, approximately 100

A Deck of Cards

For the purpose of this game, a deck of cards is Ace–10 of each of the four suits if using playing cards or four copies of each number 1–10 if using numeral cards. Remove all face cards, jokers, and wild cards. Aces remain, serving as the number 1. When complete, a deck should have 40 cards.

Players

2–4

Directions

1. Shuffle the cards and deal them out evenly to all players; set any leftover cards aside.

2. Each player stacks their cards neatly in front of them, facedown.

3. Each player then draws the top card from their stack and places it faceup next to their stack. The number on the card from their stack determines how many cubes the player will use. If using regular playing cards, Aces serve as the number 1.

4. Each player takes the corresponding number of interlocking cubes and snaps them together to form a cube stick.

5. Players compare the lengths of their cube sticks and place the sticks in order from shortest to longest.

6. Each player earns points based on the difference in the number of cubes between their stick and the next shortest stick. For example, if three players are playing and this is the scenario:

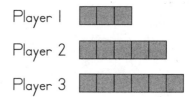

7. Player 3 has the longest stick, and it is 1 cube longer than Player 2, so Player 3 keeps 1 cube and puts the remaining cubes in her stick back in the tub. Player 2's stick is 2 cubes longer than Player 1's; therefore, Player 2 keeps 2 cubes and puts the remaining cubes in his stick back in the tub. Player 1, because she has the shortest stick, gets to keep all of the cubes in her stick.

8. In the event of a tie, meaning two or more sticks of equal cubes are created, the tied players each earn points based on the

difference in the number of cubes between their sticks and the next shortest stick. For example, if three players are playing and this is the scenario:

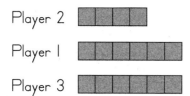

Player 2

Player 1

Player 3

9. The two players with sticks of 6 cubes have the longest sticks, which are 2 cubes longer than the shorter stick of 4 cubes. Those players each keep the difference, which is 2 cubes. The player with the shortest stick, in this scenario Player 2 with a stick of 4, keeps all 4 of her cubes.

10. While it is possible yet unlikely, there may be a time when every player has the same length of sticks (meaning they all draw the same card number). When this happens, to settle the tie, all players go back to their stack of cards and draw the next top card. They add that number onto their stick of cubes, and then recompare sticks.

11. When all of the cards are played, the game is over. To find out who is the winner, all players add up their total number of earned cubes into one stick. The player with the longest stick is the winner.

Game 9: Connect Four
(A Graphing Game)

Objective

Players alternate turns rolling the die twice. The number of the first roll determines the x-axis coordinate and the number of the second roll, the y-axis coordinate. Players record their coordinates and mark such on the game board (coordinate plane) with a colored counter. The objective is to be the first player to connect four of their colored counters in a row (horizontally, vertically, or diagonally).

Materials

- dice (labeled *1–6*)
- counters, 18 in one color and 18 in another or 36 two-color counters
- *Connect Four* Game Board (REPRODUCIBLE 12)
- pencils

Players

2

Directions

1. Decide who is Player 1 and who is Player 2. Each player selects a set of counters, ensuring that it is a different-color set than their partner's.

2. Player 1 rolls the die twice and records the numbers rolled under his column on the game board, using a comma to separate the two numbers. For the purposes of this game, these are the coordinates. The first number rolled is the x-axis coordinate and the second number rolled is the y-axis coordinate.

3. Player 1 travels along the x- and y-axes of the coordinate plane (also on the game board) and places one of his colored counters on the point where the lines intersect.

4. Player 2 repeats Steps 2 and 3, marking her point with one of her colored counters.

5. Play alternates. If a player rolls coordinates for a point that is already marked with a counter, the player loses that turn.

6. The winner is the first player to connect four of their colored counters in a row horizontally, vertically, or diagonally. Some games may end in a draw (neither player wins nor loses).

Variations
Double Marking

Instead of losing the turn when a player rolls coordinates for a point that is already marked with a counter, the player may place her counter on top of the other player's counter; this allows either player to use the intersection toward winning the game.

No Dice

Players do not play with a die but rather determine their coordinates themselves.

Game 10: Coordinates
Secrecy (A Graphing Game)

Objective

Players practice graphing points on a coordinate plane in an attempt to pinpoint secret coordinates. Players make guesses and place their guesses on the coordinate plane; the player who knows the secret coordinates records the guesses and provides information ("clues") as to whether any part of the guesses is in common with the secret coordinates. The objective of the game is to share and gain enough information to identify the secret coordinates.

Materials

- *Coordinates Secrecy* Recording Chart and Game Board 1 (REPRODUCIBLE 14)

- pencils

Players

2–4

Directions

1. Determine which player gets to choose the secret coordinates—this is Player 1. The two coordinates must be different numbers (no doubles!). Write the secret coordinates down in a place where the other players cannot see them.

2. The other player(s) make a guess at the coordinates and plot their coordinates guess on the game board (coordinate plane).

3. Player 1 reads the game board (coordinate plane) and records the guessed coordinates in the first column of the table on the game board labeled *Coordinates*.

4. Player 1 then records how many numbers are correct in the Number column and how many of those numbers are in the correct order in the Order column.

5. Repeat Steps 2 through 4 until the secret coordinates are guessed.

6. Switch roles so that a different player now becomes Player 1 and chooses the secret coordinates. Play the game again.

Variation

Game Board 2: Four Quadrants

Play a more challenging version of this game, one involving all four quadrants of a coordinate plane. Use *Coordinates Secrecy* Recording Chart and Game Board 2 (REPRODUCIBLE 15) for this game variation.

Game 11:
Coordinate Tic-Tac-Toe

Objective

This game is played much like the classic tic-tac-toe. However, in this version, players mark their moves (Xs and Os) on a coordinate plane instead of a regular tic-tac-toe board. Players take turns choosing and plotting points and then recording the coordinates of their move. The first player to get four in a row—horizontally, vertically, or diagonally—is the winner.

Materials

- *Coordinate Tic-Tac-Toe* Recording Chart and Game Board 1 (REPRODUCIBLE 16)

- pencils

Players

2

Directions

1. Players determine who will be Player 1 and who will be Player 2. Player 1 will use the symbol X and Player 2 will use the symbol O to mark their moves.

2. Player 1 decides on a move by marking X on the coordinate plane (game board). Player 1 then records the corresponding coordinates in the X column of the T-chart and reads the coordinates out loud to Player 2. Player 2 then confirms that Player 1's coordinates are correct. If the coordinates are incorrect, Player 1 is given one opportunity to correct the mistake before losing their turn.

3. Player 2 follows the same steps as Player 1, only marks her move using an O on the game board.

4. Play alternates; the first player to have four in a row—horizontally, vertically, or diagonally—is the winner.

Variations
Game Board 2: Four Quadrants

Use the *Coordinate Tic Tac Toe* Recording Chart Game Board 2 (REPRODUCIBLE 17). This game board features all four quadrants.

Four Players

Play with four players and use symbols, X, O, A, B. Note: this version requires more strategy than the two-player version.

Game 12: Desktop Shuffleboard
(A Measurement Game)

Objective

Players take turns sliding a playing card across a flat surface, like a desk or table, with the goal of getting the card as close to the opposite edge as possible without the card falling off. Players then measure and record the distance from where the card stopped to the edge of the table. After each player has had ten turns, players add up their measurements; the player with the lowest sum is the winner.

Materials

- playing card, 1 per player
- rulers
- pencils
- paper
- *Desktop Shuffleboard* Recording Sheet 2 (REPRODUCIBLE 19)

Players

2

Directions

1. Players find a flat surface (a desk or table) and clear it of all items. This surface will be the "board." Determine which side of the surface is the start side and which is the finish.

2. Players determine who will be Player 1 and who will be Player 2.

3. Player 1 places a playing card on the start side of the board, with the top edge aligned to the start edge. Player 1 firmly yet gently pushes the card so it slides forward across the surface, as if it were a disc in a game of

shuffleboard, and aims it toward the opposite end of the board. The goal is to get the card as close to the opposite edge without it falling off.

4. When the card has stopped, Player 1 then measures the distance between the card and the finish side of the table.

5. Player 2 checks Player 1's measurement; once confirmed, Player 1 records the measurement on the recording sheet.

Penalty Box

If the card falls off the board, the corresponding player adds the following "penalty" to their measurement:

- If measuring in centimeters, add 25.
- If measuring in inches, add 10.

6. Play alternates, continuing until each player has had ten turns (hence collecting ten measurements).

7. Players then each add up their measurements. The player with the lowest sum is the winner.

Game 13: Four Square
(Plotting Points)

Objective

Players each assign themselves to one of the four quadrants on the game board. The player with Quadrant I begins the game; the player rolls four dice: two with faces labeled + and − and the other two with faces labeled 1–6. The player then creates and plots a playable coordinate combination from what is rolled. Two main rules apply:

Rule 1: The coordinate pair you choose to plot cannot be in your quadrant.

Rule 2: The coordinate pair you choose to plot cannot have already been plotted.

Play continues until a player cannot plot a playable coordinate combination from his or her roll; when this is the case, all other players score a point, the game board is cleared, and a new round begins.

Materials

- dice (labeled +, +, +, −, −, −), 2
- dice (labeled 1–6), 2
- counters, 30–40
- pencils
- paper
- *Four Square* Game Board (REPRODUCIBLE 20)

Players

4

Directions

1. Players determine their quadrants on the game board (one player per quadrant) and sit/stand next to their quadrant. The player with Quadrant I always begins the game,

and per Rule 1 players cannot plot coordinates within their quadrant (just like Four Square with a bouncy ball).

2. Player 1 (Quadrant I) rolls the dice and combines the symbols and numbers to create a pair of playable coordinates. The pair of coordinates must follow two rules:

   Rule 1: The coordinate pair you choose to plot cannot be in your quadrant.

   Rule 2: The coordinate pair you choose to plot cannot have already been plotted.

3. Player 1 plots the coordinates on the game board with a counter. The other players confirm that the move is indeed a playable one.

4. The player whose turn is next is the one whose quadrant Player 1 just plotted coordinates in. This next player rolls the dice, creates a coordinate pair that abides by the two rules, and plots the coordinates on the game board with a counter.

5. The player whose turn is next is the one whose quadrant the previous player just plotted coordinates in.

6. Play continues; eventually a roll of the dice produces no coordinate combinations that can be played. When this happens, all the players but the player in play score a point.

7. Keep track of points: write each player's name on a piece of paper and place a tally mark under those players who just scored a point. When points are scored, the game is "reset"—all counters are removed from the game board and another round starts (once again, the player in Quadrant I starts).

8. Continue playing as time allows; when time is up, total your points. The player(s) with the most points is/are the winner(s).

Game 14: Geometry Go Fish

Objective

This game is a version of the classic game *Go Fish*. Players put aside pairs of cards with matching shapes. Then players take turns asking each other for shapes they need to make matching pairs. Play continues until all the cards in the deck are used up (paired) or until one player goes out by having no remaining cards to play.

Materials

- *Geometry Go Fish* Cards, 2-D Shapes (REPRODUCIBLE 22), 1 deck

Players

2–4

Directions

1. One player shuffles and deals the cards, five to each player. Place the remaining cards facedown in the middle, either in a stack or a "fishing pond" (spreading cards facedown in a pool-like array).

2. Players examine their cards. Should the shapes on any of the cards they are holding match, players place those pairs aside and draw two additional cards to replace the cards played.

3. Now players alternate turns. During turns, players ask the other players for a card that will go with a card in their hand to make a match. Two things can happen:

   - If the other player has the card requested, they must give the card to the player and that player sets the pair aside.

   - If players do not have the card being asked for, they say, "Go Fish." This means the player who requested a particular card must draw a card from the "fishing pond" or stack in the middle of the playing area.

4. A winner is determined in two ways:

   - If a player has paired all of her cards and has no cards left in her hand, she is the winner.

   - If all the cards are played and no more pairs can be made, players add up the matched cards that they have set aside; the winner is the player with the most matches.

Variation

2-D and 3-D Shapes

Play the game using cards with 3-D shapes too; to do so, add the cards from one copy of REPRODUCIBLE 23 to the mix.

Game 15: Go the Distance
(Customary Version)

Objective

Players take turns rolling two dice (labeled *1–6*) and deciding to record the sum of the rolled numbers in either inches or feet. After ten turns, the player closest to ten yards (thirty feet) without going over wins.

Materials

- dice (labeled *1–6*), 2

- pencils, 1 per player

- *Go the Distance* Recording Sheet (Customary Version) (REPRODUCIBLE 24), 1 per player

- rulers, 1 per player (optional)

Players

2

Directions

1. Decide who is Player 1 and who is Player 2.

2. Player 1 rolls the dice, adds the two numbers, and decides whether to record the sum in inches or feet on her recording sheet.

3. Player 2 rolls the dice, adds the two numbers, and decides whether to record the sum in inches or feet on his recording sheet.

4. Play alternates.

5. After each player has rolled ten times, players add up their distance (converting inches to feet as appropriate). The player closest to 10 yards (30 feet) without going over is the winner.

Variation
Going Over

Play the game with the rule that you can go over, but still remain as close to 10 yards as possible. The player closest to 10 yards (30 feet), whether over or under, is the winner.

From *Math Games for Geometry and Measurement: Games to Support Independent Practice in Math Workshop and More, Grades K–5* by Jamee Petersen. © 2019 by Houghton Mifflin Harcourt Publishing Company. Permission granted to photocopy for nonprofit use in a classroom or similar place dedicated to face-to-face educational purposes. Visit www.mathsolutions.com/myonlineresources to register your resource and download the reproducibles. See page ix for the key code.

Game 15: Go the Distance
(Metric Version)

Objective

Players take turns rolling two dice (labeled *1–6*) and deciding whether to add or multiply the numbers generated. Next, they decide to record the sum or product in millimeters or centimeters. After ten turns, the player closest to one meter without going over wins.

Materials

- dice (labeled *1–6*), 2
- pencils, 1 per player
- *Go the Distance* Recording Sheet (Metric Version) (REPRODUCIBLE 25), 1 per player
- rulers, 1 per player (optional)

Players

2

Directions

1. Decide who is Player 1 and who is Player 2.
2. Player 1 rolls the dice and then decides:
   - to add or multiply the two numbers, and
   - to record the sum or product in millimeters or centimeters on the recording sheet.
3. Player 2 rolls the dice and follows the same steps as Player 1 above.
4. Play alternates.
5. After each player has rolled ten times, players add up their distance (converting millimeters to centimeters as appropriate). The player closest to 1 meter (100 centimeters) without going over is the winner.

Variation
Going Over

Play the game with the rule that you can go over, but still remain as close to 1 meter as possible. The player closest to 1 meter (100 centimeters), whether over or under, is the winner.

Game 16: Have to Halve
(A Game of Partitioning)

Objective

Each player has a geoboard and begins by placing one large geo or rubber band around the perimeter of their geoboard to create a square. Players then take turns rolling a die to determine their next move. If a player rolls an even number, they must partition the largest section remaining in half (in the case of the first turn, this would mean partitioning the square in half) on their geoboard. If a player rolls an odd number, additional rules apply. The winner of the game is the first player to partition all the halves into half on their geoboard, creating sixteen equal parts.

Materials

- geoboard (standard 25-pegged), 1 per player
- dice (labeled *1–6*)
- geo bands or large rubber bands, approximately 12 per player

Players

2–4

Directions

1. Players sit in a circle, each with a geoboard in front of them.

2. To start, players wrap a large geo or rubber band around the perimeter of their geoboard (all twenty-five pegs) like shown here:

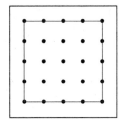

3. Players decide who will go first. Players will then take turns, in a clockwise order from the first player.

4. The first player rolls the die and refers to the *Have to Halve* Game Moves to determine the move to make:

   - *Even number:* If an even number is rolled, the player must partition the largest section on their geoboard in half.

   - *The number 1:* If a 1 is rolled, the player must remove the last band placed on their geoboard. The only exception to this is if the player rolls a 1 on their first roll, in which case they simply skip a turn as there are no bands to remove yet (beyond the starting one around the perimeter, which stays).

   - *The number 3:* If a 3 is rolled, the player skips a turn and will have to wait until their next turn to try to make a move.

   - *The number 5:* If a 5 is rolled, the order of play is reversed. (If playing with only two players, this makes no difference and just results in a no-move as if a 3 was rolled.)

Have to Halve Game Moves
If roll is . . .

- 2, 4, 6 = partition the largest section
- 1 = remove the last band placed
- 3 = loss of turn
- 5 = reverse play

5. When an even number is rolled, it's important that only the *largest* section on the geoboard gets partitioned; if a smaller section is partitioned, the player must remove the band and give up their turn until next time.

6. The first player to completely partition their geoboard—so that there are sixteen equal parts—is the winner.

Game 17: Line Plot Tic-Tac-Toe

Objective

This game is similar to the classic game of tic-tac-toe, only a line plot serves as the game board. Players take turns rolling a die to determine where they place an X on the line plot. Each time a player rolls the die, they have a choice of either:

- *playing to win:* placing an X on the line plot, above the corresponding number, or

- *playing to block:* erasing their opponent's X, if there is one above the corresponding number.

The first player to have three consecutive Xs in their color above a number on the line plot wins.

Materials

- colored pencils (with erasers or an eraser to share), each a different color, 2

- dice (labeled *1–6*)

- *Line Plot Tic-Tac-Toe* Game Board (REPRODUCIBLE 27)

Players

2

Directions

1. Decide who is Player 1 and who is Player 2. Each player selects a different-color pencil.

2. Player 1 rolls the die and, using her colored pencil, marks the number rolled with an X on the line plot.

3. Player 2 rolls the die and, using his colored pencil, marks the number rolled with an X above the corresponding number on the line plot.

4. Play alternates. From here on, each time a player rolls the die, they have a choice of either:

- *playing to win:* placing an X on the line plot, above the corresponding number, or

- *playing to block:* erasing their opponent's X, if there is one above the corresponding number.

5. The goal is to get three same-color Xs stacked on a number in the line plot. The first player to do this wins the game.

Game 18: March to the Meter

Objective

Players use two different-color game markers to "march" to the end of the meter stick. Each player rolls two dice, adds up the rolled numbers, and makes a move up the meter stick in centimeters, equivalent to the sum. Play alternates. The player who gets to the end of the meter stick (100 centimeters) or beyond first is the winner.

Materials

- meter stick
- game markers (chips, tiles, pawns, etc.), each a different color, 2
- dice (labeled *1–6*), 2
- *March to the Meter* Recording Sheet (REPRODUCIBLE 28)

Players

2

Directions

1. Decide who is Player 1 and who is Player 2. Each player selects a different-color game marker.

2. Players place their game markers at the end of the meter stick marked at the zero edge.

3. Player 1 rolls the dice, adds up the rolled numbers, and makes a move up the meter stick in centimeters, equivalent to the sum. Player 1 marks their move on the meter stick using their game marker.

4. Player 2 rolls the dice, adds up the rolled numbers, and makes a move up the meter stick in centimeters, equivalent to the sum. Player 2 marks their move on the meter stick using her game marker.

5. Play alternates. Players have the option of using the recording sheet, in addition to the meter stick, to track their moves.

6. The first player to reach the end of the meter stick (100 centimeters) or beyond is the winner.

Variations

March to the 0.5 Meter

Players follow the same procedures as in *March to the Meter*, only the winner is the player who gets to the middle of the meter stick (50 centimeters) first.

Hyper March

Add one or two more dice to be rolled each turn. Players add up all the rolled numbers and make the corresponding move on the meter stick.

Game 19: Mosaic
(An Area Game)

Objective

Players, in pairs, take turns rolling dice to generate dimensions for a rectangle. Using colored pencils (a different color per player), they then draw the rectangle on a shared piece of graph paper (the game board). Players begin the game by drawing rectangles in opposite corners of the game board. Thereafter, each time a player draws a rectangle, the rectangle must share a side or partial side with another rectangle of the same color. Eventually, players' rectangles meet near the middle. When no more rectangles can be drawn on the board, players add up the total area of the rectangles in their color. The winner is the player with the largest total area.

Materials

- centimeter graph paper, 1 sheet
- dice (labeled *1–6*), 2
- colored pencils, each a different color, 2

Players

2

Directions

1. Decide who is Player 1 and who is Player 2.

2. Each player selects a corner of the game board to begin in (corners need to be opposite of each other) as well as a colored pencil for drawing their rectangles.

3. Player 1 rolls the dice and uses the numbers to create the dimensions of a rectangle. For example, if Player 1 rolled a 3 and a 5, the dimensions of their rectangle would be 3 by 5.

4. Player 1 then draws the corresponding rectangle in their corner of the game board.

5. Player 1 labels the rectangle by writing the dimensions inside of it (Note: The only time it will be challenging to fit the dimensions inside the rectangle is if two 1s are rolled. In this case, labeling could be optional).

6. Player 2 repeats Steps 3–5, drawing a rectangle in their corner of the game board.

7. Player 2 passes the dice back to Player 1. This time, when Player 1 rolls the dice and draws the corresponding rectangle on the game board, the rectangle must be drawn such that it shares sides with the previous same-color rectangle as much as possible.

8. Player 1 labels the rectangle and passes the dice back to Player 2.

9. Player 2 now rolls the dice and draws another rectangle, only on the opposite side of the game board. This new rectangle must be drawn so it shares at least one side with the rectangle previously drawn. Player 2 labels it accordingly.

10. Play alternates. On each turn, players add a new rectangle that shares sides with a previous one.

11. The game ends when there is no longer room to draw a rectangle that shares sides with another rectangle. Players then add up all of the areas of the rectangles in their color. The player with the greatest total area is the winner.

Game 20: Positions
(Identifying and Describing Shapes)

Objective

To set up the game, a star card is placed in the middle of the playing area and four stacks of shape cards are placed faceup around the star in different positions—above, below, in front of, and behind. Players spin a spinner to determine which stack of cards to reference. They then name the shape on the top card of that stack, in addition to its position in relation to the star card. If they are correct, they earn a point and keep the card. The player with the most points (cards) wins.

Materials

- *Positions* Shape Cards (REPRODUCIBLE 30), 1 deck
- *Positions* Spinner (REPRODUCIBLE 31)
- paper clip
- pencil

A Deck of Cards

For the purpose of this game, a deck of cards consists of 49 cards: two copies each of the first four pages of **REPRODUCIBLE 30** (48 shape cards) and one copy of the star card.

Players

2 or 3

Directions

1. Decide who is Player 1, Player 2, and Player 3.

2. Find the star card in the deck of cards and place it faceup in the middle of the playing area.

3. Shuffle the remaining cards. Make four equal stacks of cards. Count; there should be 12 in each stack.

4. Place one stack faceup above the star card and another below; one to the left and the other to the right. When done, the setup should look something like this:

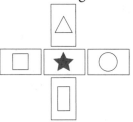

5. Players arrange themselves so they are sitting next to each other, not across. This means all players should be on the same side of the playing area.

6. Player 1 spins the spinner and announces the outcome; for example, "below."

7. Player 1 then directs her attention to the stack of cards that corresponds with the outcome—using the example in Step 6, this would mean the stack of cards *below* the star card.

8. Player 1 looks at the top card in the stack, names the shape on the card, and reinforces the position. For example, for the word below and the card with a circle on it, Player 1 would say something like, "This is a circle and it is *below* the star," or "The shape below the star is a circle."

9. If the other players agree, Player 1 sets the card aside as one point earned. If the other players don't agree, they come to a consensus as to who is right; the student ends their turn if they are wrong (no points are gained or lost).

10. Players alternate play, repeating Steps 6–9.

11. Eventually a player will take the last card from a stack. When this happens, that player earns a bonus point and the game ends. Players then count their cards, each card equating to a game point. The winner is the player with the most points.

Game 21: Roll Fives to 60
(An Analog Clock Game)

Objective

In this game, the game board is an analog clock. Players take turns rolling two dice labeled *0–5*. When a combination of five is rolled, players snap together five interlocking cubes and place them around the outside circumference of the clock, marking increments of five, starting with the first increment between 12 and 1. The first player or team to snap together twelve sets of five cubes and reach 12 o'clock again is the winner.

Materials

- die (labeled *0–5*), 2

- *Roll Fives to 60* Game Board (REPRODUCIBLE 33), 1 per player

- interlocking cubes, 60 per player

Players

2–4

Directions

1. Decide who is Player 1 (or Team 1) and who is Player 2 (or Team 2).

2. Player 1 rolls both the dice. If a combination of five is rolled, Player 1 snaps together five cubes and places them in the first five-minute increment between the 12 and the 1 on his game board clock. If a combination other than five is rolled, Player 1 loses their turn.

3. Player 2 rolls both the dice. If a combination of five is rolled, Player 2 snaps together five cubes and places them in the first five-minute increment between the 12 and the 1 on their game board clock. If a combination other than five is rolled, Player 2 loses their turn.

4. Play alternates. Each time a player rolls a combination of five, they snap together five cubes and place the stick on the next five-minute segment of the clock.

5. The first player to make it all the way around the clock, back to 12 o'clock, is the winner.

Variation
Missing Analog Clock Numbers

Use the *Roll Fives to 60* Extension Game Board (REPRODUCIBLE 34). On this game board, the numbers on the analog clock are absent. As players make their way around the clock, they fill in the numbers, recording both the hour and the number of minutes past the hour (in five-minute increments).

Game 22: Sunshine
(A Yahtzee-Like Game)

Objective

The goal of the game is to get as many points as possible by rolling like symbols according to the score sheet (*endpoints, lines, line segments, rays, parallel lines,* and *perpendicular lines*). Only one row of the score sheet can be filled in on each turn, with each turn consisting of rolling the symbol dice up to three times. The player with the most points at the end of ten turns is the winner.

Materials

- die (each face with a different symbol—endpoint, line, line segment, ray, parallel lines, and perpendicular lines), 5

- plastic or paper cup, 1

- *Sunshine* Score Sheet (REPRODUCIBLE 35), 1 per player (Note: the reproducible contains 2 score sheets)

- pencils, 1 per player

Players

2–4

Directions

1. Decide who is Player 1, 2, and so forth.

2. Player 1 places the five dice in the cup, briefly shakes the cup, and spills the dice in the middle of the playing area.

3. Player 1 looks at their score sheet and thinks, "With the current roll in mind, are there any rows on my score sheet that I am close to attaining?" For example, if three of the five dice rolled show line segments, Player 1 might want to:

   - go for the "line segment" row (with hopes of getting two more dice to land line-segment-side up within the next two rolls);

   - go for the "four of a kind" row (with hopes of getting one more die to land line-segment-side up within the next two rolls); or

   - settle on the "three of a kind" row, in which case Player 1 does not need to use their remaining two rolls.

4. If Player 1 chooses to do another roll, they place the dice aside that they want to keep and put the remaining dice back in the cup, then roll again. On each turn, players have the option of rolling the dice as many as three times. On each roll, players can set aside the dice that have generated symbols they want to keep and try again with the remaining dice.

5. After three rolls (or fewer if Player 1 chooses), Player 1 records their play on the *Sunshine* Score Sheet as follows (players can only select and fill in one row per turn!):

If a row in the top half of the score sheet is selected:

Player 1 draws the symbol in the corresponding number of boxes in that row. For example, if Player 1 chooses the line segment row and has three dice showing the line segment symbol, Player 1 draws the line segment symbol in the first three boxes of that row. Then they total up the boxes and write the number in the Total column, scoring 1 point per box (in this example, the number would be 3).

	1	2	3	4	5	total
point						
line						
line segment	╱	╱	╱			3

For the bottom half of the score sheet:

If Player 1 chooses one of the rows in the bottom half of the score sheet (players can only choose one row per turn!), Player 1 picks the row that corresponds with their play and records the points in the Total column. In the example, Player 1 might choose the "3 of a kind" row because they have three dice showing line segments.

6. Player 2 now takes their turn, repeating Steps 2–5.

7. When players fill in one of their rows, they cannot add to or change what they recorded. If they roll something that applies to a row that has already been filled in or applies to no rows, they must record a 0 in one of the yet-to-be-filled rows of their choosing on their recording sheet.

8. Play continues until each player has had ten turns (meaning all ten rows on their recording sheets are filled in, even if this means some rows have 0).

9. After ten turns, players calculate their totals on both the top and the bottom portion of the score sheets.

10. Players determine who won by reviewing each other's computations, comparing totals, and completing the three statements at the bottom of their score sheets. The player with the highest score is the winner.

Game 23A: Volume 9

Objective

Players, in pairs, create a "cube building" using 90 interlocking cubes. Players then take turns, choosing to remove one or two cubes from the top layer until the next, smaller cube building is formed. The last player to remove a cube or cubes to reveal the "new" top layer has the opportunity to identify the volume of the "new" building. If correct, the player earns a point. If the player incorrectly identifies the volume, the next player gets an opportunity to earn the point. Players continue, alternating turns and identifying the new volume of their cube building as each new top layer is revealed. The player who removes the cube or cubes revealing the original base layer and "Volume 9" earns two points. The player with the most points at the end of the game is the winner.

Materials

- interlocking cubes, 90
- paper
- pencil

Players

2

Directions

1. Decide who is Player 1 and Player 2.

2. Both players work together to create a cube building using the 90 interlocking cubes. The dimensions of the cube building should be 3 by 3 by 10.

3. Players stand their cube building up so that it is resting on a 3-by-3 side (considered the base).

4. Players take turns, choosing to remove one or two cubes from the uppermost layer.

5. The last player to remove a cube or cubes to reveal the new top layer has the opportunity to identify the volume of the new building. The player states the volume out loud. If correct, the player earns a point.

6. If the player incorrectly identifies the volume, the next player gets an opportunity to earn the point (essentially "stealing" the point from the first player).

7. Players record their points using paper and pencil.

8. Players continue, alternating turns and identifying, out loud, the new volume of their cube building as each new top layer is revealed.

9. The player who removes the cube or cubes revealing the original base layer and "Volume 9" earns two points.

10. Players total their points; the player with the most points at the end of the game is the winner.

From *Math Games for Geometry and Measurement: Games to Support Independent Practice in Math Workshop and More, Grades K–5* by Jamee Petersen. © 2019 by Houghton Mifflin Harcourt Publishing Company. Permission granted to photocopy for nonprofit use in a classroom or similar place dedicated to face-to-face educational purposes. Visit www.mathsolutions.com/myonlineresources to register your resource and download the reproducibles. See page ix for the key code.

Game 23B: Volume 25

Objective

In this version of the game, players make a "cube building" using 125 interlocking cubes (the dimensions being 5 by 5 by 5). Players then take turns, choosing to remove one, two, or three cubes from the top layer until the next, smaller cube building is formed. The last player to remove a cube or cubes to reveal the "new" top layer has the opportunity to identify the volume of the "new" building. If correct, the player earns a point. If the player incorrectly identifies the volume, the next player gets an opportunity to earn the point. Players continue, alternating turns and identifying the new volume of their cube building as each new top layer is revealed. The player who removes the final cube(s) to reveal "Volume 25" earns two points. The player with the most points at the end of the game is the winner.

Materials

- interlocking cubes, 125
- paper
- pencil

Players

2–3

Directions

1. Decide who is Player 1, Player 2, etc.

2. Players work together to create a cube building using the 125 interlocking cubes. The dimensions of the cube building should be 5 by 5 by 5.

3. Players stand their "cube building" up so that it is resting on a 5-by-5 side.

4. Players take turns, choosing to remove one, two, or three cubes from the uppermost layer.

5. The last player to remove a cube or cubes to reveal the new top layer has the opportunity to identify the volume of the new building. The player states the volume out loud. If correct, the player earns a point.

6. If the player incorrectly identifies the volume, the next player gets an opportunity to earn the point (essentially "stealing" the point from the first player).

7. Players record their points using paper and pencil.

8. Players continue, alternating turns and identifying the new volume of their cube building as each new top layer is revealed.

9. The player who removes the cube or cubes revealing the original base layer and "Volume 25" earns two points.

10. Players total their points; the player with the most points at the end of the game is the winner.